Wanna Go. Wanna Stay

My Journey in a Season of Abuse

MARIA J. SCOTT

Wanna Go. Wanna Stay: My Journey In A Season Of Abuse by Maria J. Scott
Published by Phoenix Enix Press, 3000 E. Main St., Ste. B-130, Bexley, OH 43209
www.PhoenixEnixPress.com

© 2018 Maria J. Scott
All rights reserved. No portion of this book may be reproduced in any form without permission from the author, except as permitted by U.S. copyright law. For permissions contact:
info@PhoenixEnixPress.com

ISBN: 978-0-9996009-0-0

Library of Congress Control Number: 2018948161

The events and people described in this book are real. The author has changed some dates and the names of everyone, except her parents and brother. Whenever she couldn't remember a name, she took the liberty of inventing one, hoping that she didn't accidentally use that person's real name. The conversations were written as best recalled from the author's memory.

Visit the author's website at www.MariaJScott.com

Scripture quotations are taken from *The Living Bible,* copyright © 1971. Used by permission of Tyndale House Publishers, Inc., Carol Stream, Illinois 60188. All rights reserved.

Editing by Diana DiPaolo.
Cover by Chris Cummings Designs.
Formatting by Streetlight Graphics.

Dedication

This book is dedicated to the memory of
Charles D. Scott, III,
the Encourager,
the man whom God sent into my life
after these events.

1973

Chapter 1

BEWILDERED

How did I completely miss this? It's so obvious now that he knew all along what he was going to do. But I just didn't get it that summer day in 1973.

That's when I was spending my lunch hour with Mark, my boyfriend of 13 months. Usually, we would go to one of the parks and eat at a wooden table near a garden or playground. But he stopped in a different setting this time. The silver Firebird with its black vinyl top was the lone car in a five-block grid of vacant lots in Atlanta. Some of those empty plots were shrouded in six-foot-tall weeds, while the landscape of other lots contained only large, broken cement chunks.

Mark had gotten our food before picking me up for lunch. We sat in the car munching on hot dogs smothered with cheese, mustard, and relish. All around us wavy pulses of heat rose from the street and dissipated in the air. Fortunately, he had placed two plastic cups on the console between us, so we could share a single bottle of ice-cold Coca-Cola.

The last strains of Nina Simone's song *To Be Young, Gifted, and Black* were fading on the radio, and I still basked in its message. That could have been our theme song. We were both black young adults at a time when "Black Power" shouts were regularly punctuated by raised fists, and when most of us proudly framed our faces in large, soft Afros.

Contrary to the norm, Mark wore a close-cut Afro and beard, but he exemplified black pride in his appearance and stride. He looked like a handsome, slim, six-foot tall model in his business suit and rose-tinted, rimless glasses. Even before you heard him speak, he announced his arrival with the confident click of his shoes as he walked. My height of almost 5'10" and my tailored, mini-dresses added to the mistaken impression that we might be among the up-and-coming young couples of the city.

"I finally got my program to finish without a problem today!" I jubilantly announced. "That was a real milestone because it's a big program with some complicated routines."

I was smiling, but Mark seemed distracted, so I decided not to say anything more about the project I was working on. Instead, I finished my hot dog in silence and dabbed at my mouth with a paper napkin.

"What's this about you and Dino?" he asked suddenly as he turned to face me. I was surprised at both the question and the frown on his usually pleasant, copper-colored face.

"Dino? Your *friend*, Dino? What about him?" I had met Dino at one of the classes where he and Mark taught karate to eight-year-olds.

"You're seeing Dino behind my back!"

"Dino?" I asked incredulously. "I'm not seeing Dino! You know that."

Mark's hand landed so swiftly, yet heavily, on my cheek that my body actually rose up out of the bucket seat.

Shock and rage exploded in my mind! I immediately spotted my black umbrella on the floor by my seat. I grabbed it and whacked Mark's head several times. Instead of hitting me again, he grabbed my wrists while I continued to try to hit him.

I thought the area all around the car was void of people, until

I glimpsed two men in denim overalls walking toward us. I was certain they would stop and help me. Instead, they only glanced at our battleground, smiled at each other, and kept going. They were black—brothers!—but they refused to offer to help.

Inside the car, my head whirled back toward Mark, the sense of abandonment by these total strangers making me even angrier than before.

"Let me go right now!" I screamed loud enough so the cowardly men could hear me, even though they were probably at least 10 yards away by now.

"Calm down—Calm down—Calm down, Maria!" Mark said.

"I won't be calm until you let me go!"

"OK. I am letting you go."

In spite of the calmness in his voice, his hands immediately guarded his face as he loosened the grip on my wrists. I lowered my hands, but I didn't release the big, black umbrella in my right hand.

"Give me the keys!" I shouted. My anger gave me a fierce boldness that bordered on bullying.

"You can't go back to work looking like this. Let me take you back to your place and—"

"No!" I spat the word out. "You aren't taking me anywhere!"

"OK. I will give you the keys," Mark said. "You take *me* to work." He still kept his voice low and calm as he took the keys out of the ignition.

"I'll take you to your house. You get to work the best way you can!" I said, while I yanked the keys from his hands and got out of the passenger side of my car. My eyes locked on his as we passed each other at the front of the car, the closed umbrella still gripped in my hand.

Something wet wound its way down my face as I slid into the driver's seat. Sweat? Tears? Or both? The wet saltiness coursed onto my lips. My narrowed eyes watched Mark as I laid the umbrella on my lap and started the car.

Zooming down the street, I soon emerged from the deserted neighborhood to an area that had a few buildings. It was not long before I found a familiar main road. The car tires screeched at every turn and stop sign. A quick glance told me that Mark's knuckles had brightened as his fingernails pressed into the seat cushion. I was pretty sure that the knuckles on his right hand looked similar as he grasped the door's arm rest. Neither of us had ever seen me drive like this.

Steadily he said, "You're going to have the police stopping you with that kind of noise."

I refused to look at him. "I don't care. They can arrest you when they stop me!"

Once I hit the freeway, I stomped on the accelerator, revving my car up to 75 mph, first racing down I-20 and then down I-285. *Why is it taking so long to get to his house?* I asked myself. *I want to get him out of my car.*

The freeway provided a clear view of the skies; as always, at least three planes could be seen flying away from the Atlanta airport. *I need my car to go as fast as those planes!* I thought.

The humid air surging through the open windows smothered my face, making me feel as though I were in Hades. All that stuffiness only enflamed my irritation at not yet reaching my destination.

At Mark's East Point apartment, I braked the car with a jerk, blocking off the empty parking spots in front of his building. He opened the door, then suddenly turned toward me. I defiantly faced him, daring him with two slits of eyes to stay in the car another second.

A single line of sweat trickled down his forehead, his red tie tilted slightly to the right; other than those signs, though, he still looked like a sane business person. Even his glasses remained upright on his nose.

"Maria, we need to talk," he begged.

"Get out … Of … My … Car!" I shouted.

"OK." He raised his hands in surrender.

As soon as he shut the door, my foot smashed the gas pedal, making sure the tires squealed out my anger. The Firebird and I sped away, leaving Mark standing in the parking lot.

Outside his apartment complex, I had to stop for a red light. That's when I finally peered into my rear view mirror to see just how bad I looked.

A depression on the left side of my once perfectly round Afro gave the first indication of our tussle. I could pick out the sandy-colored 'fro again until it evenly surrounded my face. But I couldn't do anything about my sanguine, puffy eyes or the large, cherry-red bruise forming on my cheek.

"I can't return to work looking this way!" I heard my own voice say.

What could I possibly tell my manager? I thought. *I had just gone out for lunch, and now I would have to take the rest of the day off. This was not how I worked a job. I would never be this irresponsible!*

And what had just happened? I have never been backhanded in the face by anybody! I have never beaten anybody on the head with an umbrella!

When I reached my apartment complex on Campbellton Road, there were only a couple of people in the parking lot and, fortunately, none of them was near my building. My heels clacked my escape up the outside metal stairwell. I ran right into the apartment bedroom, where the clock showed 1:02, past the time I would have returned from lunch normally. My mind spun, trying to remember how co-workers sounded whenever I happened to hear them call in sick over the years. I finally picked up my bedroom phone and called Southern Railway, asking for my manager's extension.

"Luke," I said in a soft voice that I hoped sounded pitiful, "I became ill while I was at lunch. I need to take the rest of the day off."

"Alright, Maria." Luke replied. "Take care of yourself."

"I will," I said weakly. "Goodbye." Inwardly, I was still trembling with anger. I was pretty sure that feeling enhanced the pitiful sound of my voice.

I hung up the phone, fighting back the army of suppressed sobs advancing up my throat. I thought I had patterned myself after my mother's ability to contain her emotions. Unfortunately, I couldn't seem to hold them back today.

The activities of the past hour felt like mismatching puzzle pieces. *This is not how my life is supposed to be!*

The slideshow of my background clicked through my head. I was raised in a Christian home where my father, the Rev. F. L. Jordan, was the respected founder and pastor of the Corinthian Missionary Baptist Church in Columbus, Ohio. Four years before, I had earned a bachelor's degree in computer science at The Ohio State University, rare for anyone in the late 1960s—more rare for females back then, and especially rare for a black female. Prior to that, I had attended Fisk University, one of the most prestigious historically black schools in America. At 26, I was a skilled programmer who had several years of experience with IBM's newest technology. I had managed to do modest travels outside the U.S., going to the Bahamas, the Virgin Islands, Puerto Rico, and Canada. Meanwhile, I still saved my money and followed my dream of moving here to Atlanta, the Black Mecca. Although I grew up in the inner city, I would either walk away from someone who was prone to fight or attempt to humor them. Consequently, I had never been in a schoolyard fight. So what was this all about?

The ringing phone interrupted my thoughts. My anger made me jerk the handset upward in order to stop its noise.

"Maria--" It was Mark.

"I do not want to talk to you! We are through!" I said firmly.

"Maria, I know you are angry, and you have every right to be—"

"I sure do. It's over between us."

I slammed down the hard plastic handset without saying anything more.

I did not need to listen to Mark's talk. I needed to think ... to figure out what to do. My father had never hit my mother. Now Mark had hit me two times, for no reason, and this one was bad. There was no way I was going to put up with this behavior.

I laid my head down on the bed as the hurt consumed every inch of my body. The bruise on my face still stung, but the real wound was the internal impact. I didn't deserve to be treated like this!

Not two minutes went by before the phone rang again. I ignored it while it squawked for attention.

Like most residential phones in that day, my phones were hard-wired into the wall. There was no way to "unplug" the phone. If you left the phone off the hook, the phone company assumed that you made a mistake, and they would make a loud, piercing noise repeat on the phone, trying to get your attention. I decided that the less intrusive sound would be to let the phone ring until Mark stopped calling.

I need to maintain my composure, I kept repeating to myself.

I need to get on with life.

I need to control my anger so that I can make rational decisions!

I finally got up and checked my face in the bathroom mirror. The oval bruise had morphed into a bluish-red patch, not as bright, but just as noticeable and twice as disgusting.

I stumbled back out of the bathroom and leaned against the wall in the short hallway, not wanting to see the evidence of our encounter and wishing that ringing phone would stop.

I really longed for someone to talk to about Mark's actions. But who?

My roommate from Fisk still lived in Atlanta. She had married two years before, so I had purposely avoided calling her often. My cousin Lena lived there with her husband and two small children, but I wouldn't feel comfortable sharing this type of problem with her. This shameful situation was something I needed to figure out on my own.

The incessant phone intrusion finally stopped.

I returned to the bedroom and sank backward onto the bed, with both palms pressing against my eyes.

I thought that things were going well for me. I had been bored and friendless in Atlanta for months before I met Mark. He not only took me to lots of places and introduced me to folks from all walks of life, but he also liked being with me almost every day. I fell in love with him. He finally fell in love with me, or so I thought. He had actually mentioned marriage. Now there would be no marriage.

I need to move on. And, unfortunately, "moving on" means that once again I would be the only lonely person in "Hot-lanta," the city where most black young adults wanted to be in the 1970s.

"Br-r-ing!" "Br-r-ing!"

The ringing phone jolted me out of my thoughts. I picked it up, hoping it was somebody other than Mark. But, realistically, who else would it be? Everybody who knew me would assume I was working at that hour.

"Maria, don't hang up on me--" As expected, it was Mark's voice.

"You don't understand that I don't want to talk to you!" I hoped my voice would convey the strength of a bulldog but, instead, a briny sob angled through my throat.

"Maria, I was just worried about losing you. I let that worry get in the way, and I hurt you. I did not mean to do what I did, and I am truly sorry."

That sob was winning the battle and, above all, I didn't want Mark to hear me crying.

My index finger stabbed the phone's switch hook, disconnecting the call, even while the handset was still at my ear. *Good! He didn't hear the sob in my throat.* I now had time to choke it back.

Chapter 2

STANDING IN THE SHADOW OF LOVE

Over the next hour, my phone rang repeatedly, but I refused to answer it. Each time it rang for several minutes, jackhammering through the peaceful refuge of my apartment with its noise.

I wanted to think through my situation. I just couldn't fathom why Mark was hitting me. No prior boyfriends had ever done that. None of my friends had ever reported their boyfriends doing this. What was going on with Mark and why? What could I have possibly done to make him act that way?

I desperately needed to talk to someone about my confusion, but I was not going to call my parents and worry them with this drama. My father counseled lots of people about various situations and, although I never heard about any adults hitting other adults, I was sure it was something I could take to a pastor. But not my father. Because he had been so strict with me for so many years, I learned not to discuss any boyfriend issues with him.

Then it hit me! Mark and I had been attending a church in a small town just outside Atlanta. Rev. Moore, the pastor, lived right here in the city. Surely I could call her for some counseling on this matter.

Just as I reached that conclusion, the phone rang again. I felt stronger now. I had someone who could help me understand what was going on. I knew I would be the victor over the sobs, so I picked up the phone.

"Maria—"

I interrupted Mark with strength and resolution exuding through my voice. "Anyone who treats me like that has nothing to say to me. Don't call me anymore. You just make me mad every time you call me! I am getting ready to call Rev. Moore because I cannot deal with a man like you!" I hung up without waiting for his response.

I knew Mark would be upset that I was going to confide in the pastor about his hitting me. Mark enjoyed a good reputation among all the people who knew him. Nobody in his circle of friends would dream that Mark could hit a woman. I was sure that Rev. Moore, too, thought his inner man matched his outward appearance and talk. I didn't care. In fact, I felt that I had trumped him for the first time that day.

I picked up the heavy Atlanta phone book and flipped through the rough pages, searching for Rev. Moore's number. Mark didn't call back this time, and I was sure that he would slither away in shame, never bothering me again.

When I called Rev. Moore's number, all I heard was the buzzz-buzzz of a busy signal.

I hung up the phone and turned on the TV, hoping she wouldn't be on her line for long.

One Life to Live. I turned the channel button. *The Young and the Restless.* Just soap operas. I never liked them. I turned off the TV and tried the radio on my nightstand.

Marvin Gaye was singing *Distant Lover*. I had to turn the radio off. *No, nobody in this apartment wants to hear about love.*

I turned the TV back on and resigned myself to watching it and the clock at the same time.

After five minutes had gone by, I tried Rev. Moore's number again. The busy signal continued to mock my efforts.

Mark wasn't calling me now, so I supposed my tactic for losing him was really working. The fact that I didn't hear from him was actually helping me to calm down a bit.

During a commercial, I brewed some tea. The rich Earl Grey tea and sweet honey smoothly rolled down my throat as I leaned back against the kitchen counter. I closed my eyes and savored its intense aroma, imagining a healing power seeping into each corner of my wounded spirit.

What a big mess! The man I love keeps accusing me of being interested in other men, and he hits me just because of his suspicions. I won't put up with that! But why would a man be so fearful of losing his woman that he would hit her?

I have enjoyed being with Mark, but it hasn't been smooth sailing. He didn't even love me at first. Then finally he did. First, he didn't have a job and had gotten behind on paying bills. Even after he got his current job, he usually had to borrow money to make it to the next payday. He didn't have any savings, so he couldn't afford another car when his sporty red TR4 fell apart. We'd been sharing my car for several months. Now this! No, as much as I didn't want to be alone in Atlanta again, this relationship ends now.

I glanced at my watch and decided to try calling Rev. Moore again.

No busy signal this time and fortunately she answered the line.

"Reverend, this is Maria, Mark's friend."

"Yes, Maria. How are you?"

"I'm not doing too well. I need to come in for counseling—as soon as possible."

"Certainly, daughter," she said, obligingly. "Can you come by this evening about 6 p.m.?"

She gave me her address and directions to her house. As I hung up the phone, I began to feel more in control of my situation, especially since Mark finally had stopped calling me.

I had a few more hours before my meeting with Rev. Moore, so I took some time to think through my options with this disastrous relationship. *If Mark leaves me alone, I will be okay. Yes, I will miss him and, yes, my heart will be broken because I do love him. Yes, I will be sitting at home alone every night. But at least I will have my self-respect.*

Self-respect by being alone again? I really miss the social life and dates that I had in Columbus. I knew lots of single people from all those years of living there.

Funny! I always thought Columbus was boring. But Atlanta, before I met Mark, far exceeded the definition of "Dullsville." I didn't have any single friends to hang out with. My evenings and weekends had consisted of reading books, trying out new recipes with my cookbook, and watching TV. No dates, no parties, just me in my nearly empty apartment.

Boredom again, or Mark? Not good options.

I've lived here—what? —a year and five months. Maybe I should leave Atlanta and go back to Columbus. That would be hard to explain to folks back home, though. Everyone knew I had been saving for three years to make this move. Friends had given me at least three or four going-away parties before I left town.

Folks would want to know why I left Atlanta in order to go back home. Before I moved there, I had sung its praises to anyone who would listen. I talked about the many black neighborhoods whose homes were far more spacious, modern, and unique than anything I had seen in the Better Homes and Garden *magazines. I told of all the handsome men my Fisk roommate had introduced me to whenever I visited her in her hometown. I voiced my delight in seeing scores of black men and women dressed in business suits, walking through downtown Atlanta at lunchtime. Plus—worst of all—I bragged that Atlanta didn't have those frigid, snowy winters like Columbus!*

I couldn't tell my friends that boyfriend problems chased me away from such an idyllic setting. Or that I was overcome with isolation in this big city. No, I am going to stay here and try to make it work for me.

Eventually, my internal debate ended, and I drifted off to sleep. When I woke up, it was almost time to see Rev. Moore. I carefully reapplied makeup to my face but, in spite of my best efforts, the bruise glowed like a highway sign lit up at night.

I got in my car and headed toward Rev. Moore's, thinking it was good that Mark and I had become regulars at her church.

Mark's friend, Andrea, a college professor, had first taken us to her little white, wood-sided church. Both Mark and I enjoyed hearing the songs and sermons of the mahogany-colored, lady pastor. We also fell in love with the folksy friendliness of the small congregation of 20 people in Gwinnett County, Georgia.

I fondly recalled the Sunday when we were invited to stay after church for dinner and sit at the pastor's table. Someone had placed two, half-inch-high squares of brown food on my plate. I picked up one square and took a bite before saying, "Um! This is delicious!" It felt rough, like cornbread, but its seasoning was spicy and much tastier than cornbread. I took several more enjoyable bites.

"What *is* this?" I finally asked.

"It's dressing!" exclaimed the lady sitting next to me. "I made it. I'm glad you like it."

Satisfaction beamed all over her smooth, caramel face. I was horrified because I was holding this square of dressing between my fingers when everybody knows you don't eat dressing with your fingers! The lady did not mention my lack of manners with her wonderful creation, but I hurriedly put the square back on my plate and reached for my fork.

The pastor's husband was sitting across the table from me. He usually had the same, uninterested expression on his face but, looking at me just then, his face cracked into a broad smile, and I thought I heard a laugh coming from his small belly. I could tell by the heat rising upward on my face that I was turning as red as the azalea bushes outside the church.

My recall of this blunder made me chuckle as I pulled into the driveway of Rev. Moore's house. I lost my mirth when I saw Mr. Moore's reaction to me that evening.

Chapter 3

SMILING FACES SOMETIMES

Mr. Moore answered my knock on the door. I was sure he tried to smother a smile as he saw the bruise on my cheek. My mind retreated from the dinner musings to the memory of the two men who had passed by my car earlier without offering to help.

Why, I asked myself, *did these men think the sight of a bruised woman was funny?*

Fortunately, Rev. Moore promptly appeared behind her husband at the door of their house.

"Hello, Maria! Come on with me."

She led the way to another small room with a desk pushed up against one wall, where a shelf of books was hanging.

"Have a seat here, Maria." She pointed to a chair that was sitting fairly close to her desk chair. "Would you like some water or lemonade to drink?"

"Oh, no thank you. I'm fine."

I glanced up at the wall just behind her and noticed the picture of Martin Luther King, President John F. Kennedy, and Bobby Kennedy. JFK was looking away. Martin and Bobby stared at me as if to ask me what I was going to do now. I quickly eyed my hands, folded in my lap, as I thought, *I don't know the answer, guys. That's why I am here today.*

"Alright!" Rev. Moore plopped down in her desk chair. "Now, tell me what you need help with."

"Rev. Moore, it's Mark."

I paused, figuring that she would be surprised that Mark was the problem. She wasn't.

"Go on," she said.

"Well, we've been dating for a little over a year now."

She nodded as though she already knew that.

I shifted in my seat before gathering up enough nerve to tell her the whole story about Mark.

"Everything had been going well in our relationship until last month. That's when he accused me of flirting with one of his friends—someone who *never* paid any attention to me. And I hadn't paid any attention to him either.

"Well, after Mark made that accusation, he slapped me. It wasn't a hard slap, but that didn't matter. I had never had anyone slap me before, and I was so shocked! Well, he immediately looked just as shocked as I was, and he apologized profusely."

She handed me a box of tissues, since tears starting falling from my eyes when I talked about the shock of the slap.

As I pulled out some tissues, I said, "I was crying, but I accepted his apologies because I knew he wasn't the kind of man to beat up on women."

I dabbed at my eyes, and went on with the story of what Mark had said and done during lunch earlier that day.

At the end of my story, more tears rushed to my eyes, but I shoved them back with the damp, scrunched-up tissues in my hand. One solitary tear got past the tissues and rolled down my cheek. I caught it just as it hung on my chin.

"I can't take those accusations and that hitting anymore from Mark."

Rev. Moore tried to hand me the box of tissues again, but I shook my head.

She had listened with interest, never changing her facial expression of pious serenity. Not once had she frowned at my report of Mark's behavior.

Rev. Moore folded her hands on the edge of the desk and leaned toward me.

"Listen. There is a simple solution to this."

I raised my eyebrows in expectancy.

She went on to enunciate each word clearly, "You and Mark need to get married."

I inhaled sharply. I had not expected that kind of advice. I wanted her to be as angry as I was and to condemn Mark's actions. I wanted her to help me understand why a man would hit a woman, and I wanted her to confirm that cutting all ties with him was the best thing for me. But that's not what she did.

She went on in a soothing voice. "Mark loves you, and you love him. God ordains marriage between two people who love each other. You two," she said with an air of finality, "just need to get married."

"Married?" I muttered the word half as a question and half as a statement because I didn't know what else to say. "I—I don't understand."

"Mark is just afraid of losing you. If you two are married, he won't be fearful anymore. He will know for sure that he has your heart."

Mark and I had one brief conversation about getting married. But here was a consult saying that we should move forward with marriage. Was that the way to solve his insecure feelings that I was going to leave him for someone else? Would the hitting really be over?

"Here," Rev. Moore reached into her desk drawer and handed

me a small, square white packet. "You should burn this in your apartment to set the atmosphere for peace."

I opened it enough to see that it contained very black incense, shaped something like fescue grass seed. I could smell a slight Persian oil aroma.

Again, this was something I didn't expect. Plenty of people in the 1970s burned incense, but it was to hide the aroma of pot—not to set the atmosphere. Confused, I thought on that while I slipped the little packet into my purse. She folded her hands together in a prayer-like pose again.

"Well…Thank you, Rev. Moore."

I was stuck to my chair. I still couldn't fully deal with what I had just heard. Nothing that day seemed like reality. Somebody else had written this weird book and plopped a 2-D version of me right into the middle of it, before slamming the pages shut.

I finally stood up, feeling that I should give her a donation or something for her time and incense. As far as I knew, church members didn't give my father donations for advice, but I didn't want to appear ungrateful.

I looked in my purse for some money while saying "Thank you" again.

When I tried to hand her a $5 bill, she unfolded her hands and pointed to a little ceramic white dish. The dish, in the shape of praying hands, had been sitting on her desk all along. I laid the money in the dish as I turned to leave.

Slowly, I drove through the city streets, trying to make sense of Rev. Moore's advice in light of our courtship over the past months.

I remembered the previous January, when Mark and I sat huddled together by the gas stove in my kitchen. The electricity had gone out during a rare Atlanta ice storm, and we were trying to stay warm under a single blanket. That's when I boldly told Mark that I had fallen in love with him. He paused, but then responded by saying, "I used to go with a woman named Della. We broke up—about a couple of months before I met you. I am still in love with her."

I was stunned speechless. Mark didn't go to a social event without having me on his arm. How *could* he be in love with someone else?

Mark went on. "You are a fantastic woman, and I really *want* to be in love with you. Once I get over Della, I'm sure you will be the one for me. Will you hang in with me 'til that happens?"

I thought about the two single black women that I had met since I moved to Atlanta. Both of them were involved with married men, and now I was finding out that Mark was not much better than a married man. *Should I tell him that I cannot be with him, knowing that he loves someone else? He has always treated me with respect. He has not flirted with other women. He spends most of his free time with me. He has always seemed proud to introduce me as "his lady." No one can tell that he doesn't care for me as much as I do for him.*

My inner thoughts tumbled on, sorting through the implications and ramifications of Mark's declaration. Then I thought about how his response showed the difference between him and other men I had dated.

When we first met, I was struck by how passionate Mark talked about this country's treatment of the downtrodden. I attributed that fervor to Mark being a decade older than me and more aware of the inequities of society. Was that age difference kicking in here? Most men I dated wouldn't admit that they loved someone else. They probably would say, "I like you—a lot. It's just that 'love' is too strong a word to use right now." But no, Mark went all the way by telling me why he didn't love me! Well, I needed to go all the way and figure out if I should continue investing my time in him.

"What if you get back with Della after all these months? Where does that leave me?" I asked.

"I doubt that will ever happen. I have not seen her since the day we broke up. She doesn't call me and I don't call her." He sighed. "It's over. I just haven't gotten her out of my system yet."

Neither of us spoke for a minute or so.

I knew I honestly didn't want to go back to my boring life before I met Mark, so I finally broke the silence.

"Yes, I'll hang in with you," I said, earnestly hoping that someday Mark would fall out of love with her and fall in love with me.

His lips lightly brushed my forehead. I planned to never mention Della again, in hopes that Mark would never think of her again.

Just two weeks later, Mark and I were cleaning out one of the closets in his apartment. He had to leave for a meeting, and I volunteered to stay with the job of either filing important papers or throwing out the ones that were no longer of any use.

I reached in the closet and pulled out a pink envelope that simply said "Mark." Then I opened the matching paper inside in order to determine its value. The name at the bottom of the letter stabbed me in my heart and told me that I should read it.

Dear Mark,

Even before we proclaimed our love for each other, I was convinced you were the man for me. I wish you understood just how much I love you and want to be with you—always. Together, I know that we can conquer the world and all the obstacles that it puts in the way of strong black men.

I will stop by on my way home from work tomorrow. Oh yes, we've got to do something about those marks on my body. I cannot be walking around with them.

I love you.

Della

This was the "Della" that he was still in love with! She was proclaiming her love for him and chiding him for the love bites on her neck from some intense lovemaking session they had.

That was not a letter that I wanted him to re-read. I tore it and the envelope into four pieces and shoved them far underneath the other papers in the trash bags.

Della's letter had literally screamed a warning at me. But I still missed that warning as my mind went on to the day when Mark walked up behind me, tenderly wrapped his arms around my waist, and finally whispered in my ear, "I love you."

I had rejoiced that Della's hold on Mark was broken, but now I had another problem. Was Rev. Moore's solution really going to stop Mark's jealousy? And did Mark even *want* to get married to me?

Chapter 4

WE CAN WORK IT OUT

I PONDERED THOSE QUESTIONS FOR A few minutes after I arrived back in the parking lot of my apartment building. When I finally walked up the stairs and opened my door, I was greeted by the sound of a ringing phone.

The closest room to the front door was the kitchen, and that's where I picked up the wall phone.

"Maria, what did Rev. Moore say?" It was Mark, rushing his words.

How did he know that we had just talked? I only told him that I was going to call her. I didn't tell him that I'd gotten an appointment. And why did he start calling again, after he had stopped calling for several hours?

"Well-l-l…" I dragged that word out as I debated whether I should tell him what Rev. Moore said. The fact was that he had only said that "one day" he would ask me to marry him. There had been no indication that "the day" had arrived.

Finally, I decided to say it, but I still said it with an air of disbelief. "She said we should get married!"

"And we should!" He was not the least bit surprised. Instead, he kept talking. "I want to marry you. I love you, and I promise you that I will honor and cherish you for being the woman of my dreams. Will you marry me?"

There it was. The excited proposal—the reciprocation of my love—that I had longed for ever since he had told me he was in love with Della. This day, though, my response was not excited.

"Mark. Ah. I need to think about this."

"What's there to think about? We love each other. I almost lost you today, and I realized that I was just being stupid, real stupid. I need to make this right. *We* need to make this right. Let's get married."

I sighed. "We can't."

"Why not?"

"Well, for one thing, you're still married."

I had learned to ask potential dates early on if they were married. That's how I knew that Mark's wife was a grad student, who had walked out on him three years before. Neither had ever gotten a divorce. He was certain that she had left town, but he said he had no idea where she had moved.

"I won't be married in three weeks," he countered.

I gasped. "What do you mean?"

"I got the divorce papers in the mail a couple of weeks after I talked to my wife," he said. "I signed them and sent them back to the attorney. The divorce is final in three weeks!"

His wife had called him a few months back when I was at his house. She told him she had filed for a divorce, but that didn't bother him. What did bother him was that, while loudly expressing her anger, she told him she was pregnant when she left him and that she was going to tell their son that his father was dead. She declared that he would never meet the boy or even know his name. A curtain of sadness had drawn over Mark's face after that call. I had tried to comfort him but, for a couple of hours, he waved me away so that he could be alone in his sorrow. Now I was finding out about the real aftermath.

"You never told me about the divorce papers!" I said.

"No, but I'm telling you now. We can get married!"

"Mark, I don't think so." I said slowly, still trying to process what he was telling me.

"Did I lose you, Maria? Did I make you stop loving me?"

"I still love you, but … ," I said hesitantly.

"But what?"

"I just can't trust you, Mark. You told me before that you would never hit me again,"

"Are you saying that I can never earn your trust again?"

"Mark, I don't know!"

"Do you want to be with somebody else now? Do you want to date other people?"

"No, of course not!" I exclaimed.

The thought of trying to rev up a social life again came back to me. *I didn't mean to sound so desperate when I answered his question. I never told Mark about the loneliness I experienced before I met him. He doesn't know how much I appreciated that he took me to so many Atlanta events, introduced me to scores of people and, in general, occupied all my leisure moments with activities that were enjoyable just because we were together.*

"I don't want to date anyone else either!" he said. "You have shown me what a beautiful black queen you are. I know you are a faithful woman, so let me give you the royal treatment you deserve."

I was still confused. *When Mark wasn't accusing me of being unfaithful, he did treat me like a lady.* I pulled out the white packet of incense from my purse and ran my thumb across the rough, black particles inside.

I love this man, and he is literally begging me to be his wife. It's been months since I first told him I loved him. Why am I turning him down when I finally have his love—and a marriage proposal? Maybe … we can make this relationship work.

"Three weeks," he said. "Let's get married then! What date is that? The 27th! Come on. Let's do it on that day!"

He sounded just like a little kid running through the front gates of Disney World. I felt like the parent trying to keep up with a child who was dragging me into the theme park.

"Come on, Maria. Be my wife. I love you. If you'll become Mrs. Mark Towns, I'll make you the happiest woman on earth. I promise. Come on!"

I chuckled at his exuberance. *A happy marriage is what I really wanted, not the loneliness of being single in Atlanta. Mark really wants to be married to me, so how can he doubt my faithfulness if we get married? This is now the third time he has said that he loved me. I have to believe that our future happiness is worth making the effort.*

"Okay," I said. Then I laughed. "Okay. Okay."

"Great! Three weeks from today?"

I looked up at my wall calendar. "No, that's a Tuesday. We should do it on a Friday so we have a long weekend to honeymoon."

"OK! Then the first Friday after that," he declared. "What date is that?"

"The 31st."

"We'll do it on the 31st!" He sounded so happy. "I promise you won't regret it!"

I was happy, too. Stuffing a nagging warning deep in the back of my head, I hoped he was right about "no regrets"—on his part or on mine.

Chapter 5

LOVIN' YOU

By the next day, the bruise on my cheek had ripened into an eggplant purple color. I again tried covering it up with makeup, but that only buffed up the spot, making it the most noticeable thing on my face. I called in sick that day. I also hummed and sang through my day, as I was happy to know that I would soon be Mark's wife.

Early in the afternoon, I walked across the parking lot to the collection of apartment mailboxes. The only mail I had was a letter from Kirk. Immediately, a wave of guilt consumed my body, all the way down to my toes. I carried the letter back to my apartment, remembering how I reconnected with Kirk.

The peaceful civil rights protests of the 1960s had evolved in the 1970s to "employ-any-means-necessary-even-if-it-turns-violent." Although Mark didn't have any guns, he believed that blacks would only gain their rights by taking them. He sincerely believed that a revolution was on the horizon. Since his closest friends championed the same beliefs, he usually knew about any black activist events in Atlanta.

One Saturday, right after we started dating, Mark and I sat on hard, wooden gymnasium bleachers with at least 100 other people for a seminar. The speakers talked about how the federal government had directed violent or punitive actions toward blacks who showed leadership in this new movement.

One of the speakers at this seminar was Sheila, a petite, 30-something woman whose house Mark and I had visited. When Sheila was introduced, I was surprised to hear that she had been a brave and significant leader in the civil rights demonstrations in Atlanta in the '60s.

Sheila's call to action was that the black community needed to encourage all those who were incarcerated.

"I am specifically appealing to you today on behalf of the brothers and sisters who are activists," she said, "But I also want to remind you that there are many others in prison who are not political prisoners.

"Some have been falsely accused and imprisoned just because 'we all look alike,' so they are paying the price for someone else's crime."

She proposed that we keep a flow of encouraging letters to those in jail. Sheila had a list of incarcerated activists, and I was planning to ask for that list until she went on speaking.

"Some of those in prison did illegal activities that had nothing to do with our rights. They were legitimately sentenced to jail time."

Sheila went on. "If you know someone who is in jail, I am asking you to make sure you stay in contact with them. Let them know that they have not been forgotten. Send them letters and keep the correspondence going."

Why, Kirk is in jail—right here in Atlanta, I thought, *and I have never contacted him. How can I proclaim that we should remember those in jail when I haven't even remembered him?*

His charges were valid because he was a burglar. Still, that was not a good reason for not thinking about him, especially since everyone else in his immediate family was too far away to even visit.

As we left the event, I made a sheepish admission to Mark.

"I had forgotten until Sheila's speech that I have a cousin who is in the Atlanta Penitentiary."

"You do? How long has he been there?"

"I don't know. Maybe four or five years. I heard about it at the time he was sentenced, while I was still living in Columbus. But I never thought about it again until today. Sheila's words had me fired up about the political prisoners, but then when she mentioned the fact that we shouldn't forget the nonpolitical prisoners, I was ashamed of the fact that I had forgotten about him in all this time since I've been here."

He briefly peered at me while letting down the black convertible top of his car. "Yeah. That's almost criminal, Maria."

"I know. I am going to see if I can get his address and, if so, I'll write to him."

My cousin Kirk was four or five years older than me. He had lived in Buffalo, New York, so I only saw him during his very rare trips to Columbus. The last time I saw him, I had been a teenager, and he was in his early 20s.

I remembered that he had skin the color of milk chocolate and hazel eyes. He was so handsome that my teenaged girl friends and I were in awe of him. Would he remember the skinny teenager from those days?

I eventually got Kirk's address from relatives and found out that he did remember me. He told me that he spent most of his time either playing his trumpet or reading books that I wouldn't dream of touching. Books authored by people like Mao Zedong or Frantz Fanon or Che Guevara. These were some of the same books that Mark enjoyed reading.

Kirk's first letter was my introduction to life behind bars:

> *There are all types of people locked up here in the Pen.*
>
> *Some of them are very intelligent men. Sometimes they are in legitimate businesses and just did some illegal*

> dealings. Others used their smarts to get involved in illegitimate businesses. And then there are the hard-core, bona fide mobsters. I stay friends with all of them.
>
> Then there are the inmates who are just jerks. They think they are smart, but they aren't about anything. They complain about what's happened to them, even though it's of their own doing. And they don't want anybody else to be reasonably happy.
>
> You know, I just play my horn and don't bother anybody. But these fools will come along and loud-talk me while I'm playing in my cell. They'll say that what I'm playing is junk. They can't understand jazz, so they call it junk.
>
> I keep playing anyhow because I know my music has a message.

It sounded as if Kirk had mellowed in his adulthood. He was more serious than the kid who was repeatedly sent to reformatories or local jails for stick-ups or burglaries.

In his first letter, Kirk asked me to apply for a visitor's permit so that I could visit him. I had visited him at the Pen three or four times so far, and he really seemed to have matured in his outlook on life.

Now, as I re-entered my apartment, I calculated that it had been two months since my last visit to the penitentiary. I sat on my bed and opened the letter, knowing that Kirk would ask two things: why he hadn't heard from me and when my next visit would be.

> Dear Maria, At long last, my parole's been granted!....

My guilt over not visiting instantly converted into happiness for Kirk. My eyes raced through the rest of the words on the letter as I hadn't expected this day to come so soon. Well, it wasn't really that soon for Kirk.

His latest letter ended with the expected plea.

> *Come back and see me before I get out.*

There was also another request.

> *Would you pick me up in front of the Pen at 9 a.m. on my parole date? They'll give me a bus ticket home, but I'll need a ride to the bus terminal. Let me know if you can do that when you visit again.*

The parole date was still a couple of months away, so I gladly made plans for my last visit to the Atlanta Penitentiary. I couldn't wait to tell Kirk about our wedding plans.

With the wedding date just around corner, Mark suggested that it be just the two of us at Rev. Moore's house.

"Did you tell your mother that we were getting married?" I asked Mark several days later, while he was sitting at his dining table reading and sipping tea. Mark's two white standard poodles, Leta and her daughter Hasana, were resting by the table. I was in his narrow kitchen preparing a pot roast.

He looked at me through the pass-through. "Yes, I did tell her."

"What did she say?"

"She said something like, 'You know what marriage is, and you know what you will need to do.'"

"That's all?"

Mark nodded and went back to reading his book. I was a little disappointed because I thought Mrs. Towns liked me. I had been hoping for her to be excited. But I hid my disappointment and kept on with my cooking.

Then I heard Mark's voice again.

"You know, I probably won't tell anybody that we got married. We'll just be…married." He chuckled on that last word.

I looked at him, with thoughts swirling through my head. *The mid-70s were a time when people had started saying they didn't need a marriage license to show that they were committed to each other. More and more people were living together in lieu of getting married. But weren't we doing this so that he would know for certain I was his? Wouldn't he want all his male friends to know that, so he wouldn't think they were trying to date me?*

Unfortunately, some of his friends already thought we were living together, since I was at his apartment so often. Admittedly, I was at his place more than I should have been, but I had no intention of moving in without being married. I tried to justify my actions because I had no real furniture other than a bedroom suite, because Mark had a fully furnished apartment, because I was a dog lover who enjoyed being around his two pets, and because I could spend more time with the man I loved.

I turned back again to seasoning the pot roast without making any verbal response. While I thought his declaration was very odd, my only real concern was for Mark to feel secure in the knowledge that I was faithful to him.

My parents had been surprised to know that I wanted to get married in a small private ceremony in Atlanta, instead of having a big church wedding at home. I found out later that Dad asked Mama if I was pregnant after I told them what we were doing. I should have realized that would be a natural thought about a "quickie" wedding. I didn't want to tell them that I was only trying to get married fast so that we could move past Mark's newfound jealousy.

Chapter 6

JOY AND PAIN

Paw-Daddy, Muz, Boon-Boon, and Gan-Gan—those were the names for my grandparents whom I was closest to. My mother had called her parents "Paw-Daddy" and "Muz," a holdover from her early childhood when her own grandparents raised her. Paw-Daddy and Muz had divorced and remarried, and the other two nicknames were for their second spouses. "Boon-Boon" was a product of me, during my baby days, trying to say "Bloomer," my grandfather's last name, which was the name that Muz called him. "Gan-Gan" was the name that stuck from my trying to say "Granny."

During our last phone call, Mama told me that Gan-Gan had a stroke and, since Paw-Daddy had died years ago, she was staying with her sister while recuperating. I hurriedly made plans for a day trip to see her before our wedding. The drive to Bowling Green, Kentucky, took 10 hours round-trip, so I was pleased when Mark said he would take off work and help me with the drive to see Gan-Gan.

Unfortunately, my air conditioner had gone out in my car long ago and, because Mark was always borrowing a little extra cash, I didn't have enough money to get it fixed. Atlanta felt like a sauna that day but, since we would be on the highway for most of the trip, I hoped that the air from the open windows would cool us down somewhat.

I drove first, with a plan for both of us to drive halfway to and from Bowling Green.

Leaning my left elbow on the window sill, I glided down the freeway, enjoying the opportunity for highway driving again.

I wondered how to best prepare myself for my grandmother's condition. I didn't know much about strokes, but I had seen that it often left people bedridden, and sometimes they weren't able to move one side of their bodies. I had never seen Gan-Gan as anything except vibrant and fun. Now I had to shore up my feelings in advance so that I would be upbeat the whole time I was in her presence.

I had driven about an hour when Mark sighed heavily and said, "I see what you're doing."

Puzzled, I said, "What?"

"You and that driver. You two are making hand signals to each other, then going back and forth passing one another."

"What?" I said, completely dumbfounded by his statement.

"Mark," I said as calmly as possible, "I have no idea which driver you are talking about, and I surely wouldn't pick some *stranger* on the road to flirt with."

He grunted softly, and I silently hoped that he wouldn't lose his temper while we were on our way to my grandmother's. Fortunately, he said no more about it, and the rest of the drive went well. Unfortunately, I didn't recoil at this sign that Mark still was having trouble with his jealousy, even though we were so close to the wedding date. I should have backed out of the wedding as soon as I got home, but my desire to get married blocked out any wisdom that I should have had.

By the time we reached Bowling Green, Mark was driving. When he pulled up into the driveway of my aunt's house, I saw my grandmother standing just inside the screen door, smiling and leaning on a cane. She had never been on a cane before, but that didn't matter. She was standing and still able to walk, and she was waiting for me!

"There's Gan-Gan!" I squealed, jumping out of the car almost before it came to a stop and running up the stoop to hug her.

Meanwhile, my childish excitement caused Mark to smile and chuckle repeatedly. Her speech was normal, and her hearty laughter bubbled over us; the only thing different was the cane. I wanted to hop up and down with pleasure, but I contained the impulse in my legs.

We had a wonderful visit with Gan-Gan, my great-aunt, and her husband that day. We ate fried chicken, potato salad, and homemade cake. And we talked constantly, until it was time for us to make the five-hour drive back to Atlanta. On the trip home, Mark chuckled at me as I kept talking about how it was such a wonderful day and how I was glad he came with me. My excitement over my grandmother's condition overshadowed everything else that evening.

I didn't have a clue that I would never see Gan-Gan alive again. She died just a few days later.

Chapter 7

I'M SO INTO YOU

Mark and I were married at Rev. Moore's house on a hot and humid Friday. I wore a cream-colored suit, while Mark looked extremely handsome in a gray suit, white shirt, and deep rose-colored tie. Neither of us had any money for new outfits, but we had paid someone to make us customized, matching wedding bands. We picked out symbols to surround the bands: a heart, an ankh, a cross, and an olive branch to symbolize the life, peace, sanctity, and love in our marriage. Mark surprised me with a pink rose corsage which he pinned on my jacket before we left my house.

I officially moved into Mark's apartment. Mark's brothers came over to help move my bedroom suite into storage, since there really wasn't any more room in Mark's apartment for that. To my surprise, Mark told everyone in our social circle that we had gotten married.

For our first few weeks of marriage, it was smooth sailing. Now our combined incomes went toward the expense of only one apartment. We were close to riding on a financial high—as soon as we covered a few last bills belonging to Mark.

The only damper was that I learned my grandmother, Muz, had been diagnosed with terminal cancer. I had just taken my allotted vacation for the trip to Bowling Green and for our short stay-at-home honeymoon time. I prayed Muz could hang on until I accrued some more vacation time because I really needed to see her.

In late September, my manager, Luke, called me on a Saturday to let me know that one of my computer programs had stopped running unexpectedly. This was not odd. Once new programs went from test mode into production, it was always the programmer's job to get them running if they should end abnormally.

"Can you meet me at the office so we can figure out what went wrong and get it working again?" Luke asked.

"Sure. I'll meet you in half an hour."

I explained to Mark what was going on. Surprisingly, he said, "I'll go with you."

"Mark, it will be very boring for you. All we're going to do is look at dumps—uh, reams and reams of papers with lots of rows and columns of hexadecimal data."

"What does that do for you?"

"Well, dumps actually are similar to black boxes after a plane crash. They basically show how the internal data looked at the time the program abnormally ended."

"Yeah?"

"Yeah. So when I'm looking at the dump, I'm trying to figure out one of two things. Was the data bad? Or if the data was really supposed to look that way, what should the program have done with that good data?

"Either way, figuring that stuff out is mostly quiet analysis and investigation. And once I figure it out, I need to write the correct code into the program and have the operator run the program again. And then I have to wait to make sure that the program will run to completion with my fix in it."

"Well, I still want to go and see this."

"Okay," I sighed.

When we got to the office, I introduced Mark to Luke. He

directed us into the windowed conference room where he had already laid the foot-high stack of dumps.

Luke and I spread out the green and white, continuous-print pages as we started looking for the data that had tripped up my program.

Neither Mark nor Luke was going to be much help. Mark didn't know a thing about programming. With a cigarette in one hand, he randomly flipped through a stack of pages, looking at the hexadecimal numbers as though he were going to figure something out.

A couple of hours dragged by before Steve, my project leader, poked his head through the door of the conference room. On work days, Steve always wore a tucked-in shirt and tie. On this Saturday, he was wearing scruffy jeans and a long shirt top that fell almost to his knees.

"The computer room alerted me to the problem, so I thought I'd come in and see what I could do to help," he announced.

Poor Steve! I knew he probably didn't want to be there. He had a wife and small kids, and I was sure he would rather be spending time with them on a Saturday afternoon.

But here he was, coming in to help. He asked some questions about the problem I was seeing. Then he, too, began studying some of the data in the dumps. Between his questions and my input, we excitedly figured out what was wrong, fixed it, and were all able to go home before nightfall.

"How long has Steve been working there?" Mark asked while he was driving us home.

"Um. I have no idea. He was already there when I started working on the project last year." Wearily, I leaned my head back on the seat.

"You like him?" Mark asked.

"Yeah. He's nice, pretty laid back."

"He ever try to hit on you?"

"Naw. Steve is married." I kind of chuckled at the thought of Steve getting romantic with anybody.

"He's got a beard."

"Yeah. I always thought he looked like a hippie."

"You and Steve been seeing each other?"

"What?" I sat up straight.

"You like beards."

Now I was indignant. "No, I do not like beards!" Then I remembered that Mark had a beard.

"You are the only man I've *ever* dated who had a beard!"

Maybe Mark was worn out, too, from all the hours we just spent at my job. He fell silent and didn't say another word about Steve. The probability of me never having a program abnormally terminate on the weekends or some evening was almost nil. I wondered if he was going to be concerned about Steve every single time it happened.

Mark had enough concerns about his own job. He was working as a tenant counselor at one of Atlanta's housing projects. This was a job that he loved and put a lot of time and energy into.

"She wants to run the place!" Mark complained later that same week. He was talking about his co-worker in his office.

I was in my blue robe, setting up my typewriter on the dining table so that I could complete the newsletter that Mark decided to create for the tenants in his projects. He came up with the topics, but he had enlisted me as the interviewer and the copywriter. My final task was to type the finished newsletter on the mimeograph stencil, after which Mark would run the copies off at the Atlanta Housing Authority office.

"Is she your boss?" I asked, referring to his co-worker.

"No!"

"Are you her boss?"

"No. We both have the same job title."

"OK, but it sounds like she has been there a while."

"Yeah, she's been there at least five years. Maybe longer."

"So you're the new guy on the block."

"Yeah, but that's why they brought new people in to these projects. To get away from doing the same thing over and over again."

"So is she trying to block anything that you're trying to do?"

"Yes. She has something negative to say about anything that I do."

"Does she stop you from doing anything?"

"No. But I have to listen to her talk about how this won't work or how I should do it her way."

"And have you talked to your real supervisor about that?"

"No. I don't want it to seem like there's friction already."

"Then you need to try to work around the negative comments."

"Can't."

"Yes, you can. You have style and finesse. You could smile at her and say something like, 'Well, I want to try this and see how it works. If it doesn't work, I'll try another idea.'"

"You don't know this lady. She'll just keep on with her comments."

"Well, you want to do everything you can to get along. Did you try asking her if she needed some help with some of her projects?"

He scoffed. "No. I'm not going to do that!"

"Well, what are you going to do?"

"I don't know. I'll think of something."

He took out his consolers: pale, yellow joint papers and a small bag of grass. I had learned on our first date that Mark smoked weed. Prior to that day, I had never been around anyone who smoked marijuana. Although I was repelled by the heavy, obnoxious smell and the inhaling sniff that reminded me of a child at the tail end of a cry, I chose to ignore those turn-offs.

"I'll make it work one way or another," Mark reiterated as he prepared to smoke his joint.

Going forward, I heard fewer complaints about his co-worker as Mark continued to think up new ideas for his tenants.

It was more important than Mark realized that he and his co-worker got along well. Mark had been waiting to be called to a drug counseling job when I met him. After the funding fell through, he kept searching for something else that would allow him to do community service in black neighborhoods. That's when I found out that Mark never completed his college education.

I knew he had some college background from when he said his sister's selection as a fraternity queen was due to his influence while on campus. When I expressed surprise that he had joined a frat, he said that he had not. Instead, he insisted that it was because of the respect the fraternity had for him that they picked his personable and beautiful sister as their queen.

Mark had spent time in the Army, so I knew that he could get financial help for his schooling.

"Mark, you know that most of those types of jobs you want require psychology or sociology degrees," I told him. "Why don't you consider going back to college and finishing up a degree?"

He blew out the smoke from his cigarette and shook his head vigorously. "I once posed a question to my professor, and he could not answer it. He's supposed to be teaching me, but he cannot answer my questions. That meant he knew less than I did. That's when I realized there was no reason to continue my education.

"I've already been educated way past those types of degrees. I've lived in the community. I know their frustrations and needs better than the degreed people who have never lived in the ghetto."

I frowned as I stroked Leta behind the ear. A college degree was something my family always pushed. It was a way to get ahead. We knew that as black people, we had to be better than a white person in order to be considered for a job. That meant we had to at least have a college degree if the job called for one.

Mark continued preaching his philosophy on college, while

waving his hands around the living room and dining area. "Plus, think about this: all the books I've read exceed everything being covered in those four-year programs."

He did have neat stacks of books in every room, and he had read all of them. He had the writings from philosophers of old, like Plato and Aristotle. There were many more books from the newer guard: Karl Marx, Melville Herskovits, Lerone Bennett, James Baldwin, and others.

Mark went on with his discourse about college professors. "There's nothing new they could tell me that I don't already know. No, I don't need to go back to college. These community program directors need to understand what kinds of minds they should hire!"

I tucked away that college suggestion in the back of my mind. If things didn't work out in the job market, I could always bring it back out again.

Mark eventually got a job with the Atlanta Housing Authority. Every time he mentioned a problem with his co-worker, I kept praying that the two of them would work around their differences so he could keep on at this job that he enjoyed so much.

Chapter 8

WHERE IS THE LOVE?

THE PHONE RANG WHILE MARK and I were in the bedroom watching TV one evening a few days later. Mark picked up the phone as always.

"Maria? Yes, she's here."

He handed the phone to me and stood beside me, hands on his slim hips, grimly watching me while I answered it.

"Hello?"

"Hi, Maria," said the voice on the other end. "This is Jess from the computer room. This program HA7280 abended with an error code of P0119. We need you to fix it so it can run to completion."

I had stood up to answer the phone, but now I sat down on the bed, analyzing the information Jess had given me. "OK. Well, that code means the header record didn't agree with the rest of the data. Can you count the number of cards in the batch?"

"Sure. Hold on."

I heard the muffled clatter of cards running through the card counter before he came back with the result. "There're 145 cards."

"OK. Now, Jess, can you look at the first input card and read the numbers back to me, please?"

Jess read the information, and I was relieved that it would be a simple fix.

"Alright. We need to create a replacement card for that first card. Make up a new card that has everything else the same except the number 145 in columns 3 through 5. Got that?"

"Yeah."

"I'm going to stay on the phone while you make the change and run that batch through again."

Jess put down the phone and went away for a couple of minutes. I noticed that Mark was still standing beside me, as he had been when he handed me the phone.

I smiled up at him because I was sure this action would fix the problem without me having to go in to work that night. He did not return the smile. Instead, he walked quickly out of the room, with the dogs following him.

Jess returned to the phone. "OK. I made the change and started it up again."

"Good."

We waited for five minutes. Meanwhile, Mark had returned to the room and fixed his eyes on me, while he continued to stand on the other side of the bed. Every now and then, Jess would give me a status like "It started up," "We're coming to the time where it stopped before," or "I think we've gotten past that stopping point."

Finally, Jess declared, "And that did it! It ran to completion and started up the next job. I think we're good here. Thanks a lot, Maria!"

"Sure. I'm glad it was something simple."

As I hung up the phone, Mark walked closer to where I sat.

"What was that all about?"

"Whew! That was one of the guys from the computer room. There was a problem with my program but, fortunately, it was something that we could fix over the phone." I leaned back, with both my hands resting on the bed, feeling pleased with how we'd handled the problem.

I wondered to myself, *Where did Leta and Hasana go?*

"It didn't sound like that," Mark said. "It sounded like you two were setting up a meeting somewhere."

"Aw, come on, Mark. There's no way you could have gotten that out of our conversation."

"Oh yeah? You were speaking in code, but both of you knew what that code meant."

"Mark, we were fixing the data on one of the cards."

With a sudden single bound, Mark straddled my torso, knocking me backward on the bed. Both of his hands encircled my neck.

I couldn't get any words out to tell him to stop. I also couldn't breathe. Kicking wasn't having any effect because his body was positioned above my legs. He was yelling at me, but the words were lost in a tunnel somewhere. I didn't need to hear; I needed to breathe. I frantically pulled at his wrists so that I could loosen his grip on my neck. His arms weren't budging. I was completely out of breath. I needed to pull harder, or else I was going to die!

Miraculously, Mark stopped strangling me and jumped up off the bed.

"You're lying! You're lying!" He was standing in front of me, yelling.

I sat up and gasped a big gulp of air, then threw both hands on my chest as I coughed—big rasping hacks—over and over again.

Mark was still ranting. "You're lying to me. That man is your boyfriend! Say it!"

I couldn't even answer him because I was trying desperately to get some of that precious air back into my lungs. He just stood there, continuing to yell accusations at me.

Finally, Mark stopped talking and went to get a cigarette. He came back into the bedroom and sat down in the chair, while he lit the cigarette. I was still trying to recover.

"I cannot trust you for one minute," he said. "Who was that?"

I was leaning over the side of the bed. I managed a weak, raspy reply. "It was the computer operator from my job."

"So that's who you are seeing?"

"No." The coughing continued to shake my body. "I had a problem with my program. Just like I did the day you and I went in to the office."

"How come it's always *your* program that needs to be fixed?"

I felt drained from the coughing, but I needed Mark to get calm.

"It's a new program." Leaning over and holding my forehead with my hands, I groaned out the words. "It takes a while to work through all the kinks."

"Likely story!" Mark looked at the TV and said nothing else to me.

While he sat in silence, I tried recovering from my near-death experience, all the while thinking about the seriousness of the situation.

Marrying Mark is not the answer to his problem. He is going to continue being jealous for no reason at all. And he is going to continue to act on his suspicions. I need to do something else!

Chapter 9

A CHANGE IS GONNA COME

THE NEXT MORNING AT WORK, my eyes played tug of war with my brain. I tried to concentrate on the page of programming code I was writing, but I couldn't keep my eyes from looking up at the wall clock in the office every few minutes. It was now 9:30 a.m., and I had to wait until my manager's meeting was over at 10. I still didn't have a fully conceived plan, but I knew I needed to do the right thing by my employer.

Think! Think about this code! I told myself repeatedly.

It was useless. It was only the start of a new program, and now somebody else would have to finish it. Probably the most expedient thing for them to do was to start fresh. I didn't want anyone else in our office to know how conflicted I was, so I stared at the coding pad again and willed myself to finish at least another half page of code. I pulled the flow chart closer and started writing code again.

It's 9:40 a.m. When did time ever move so slowly?

Cathy, who occupied the desk in front of mine, turned around in her seat, as she often did, so she could face me.

"Ugh! I cannot figure this out," she said. "I need to get these tables to line up on my print, and they are not doing it. Can you take a look at what I'm doing?"

Both of Cathy's innocent eyebrows had risen on her freckled face. I was glad for the distraction—any distraction. Looking over her problem and offering a suggestion took up most of the remaining time. It was now 10 o'clock. Time to do this!

I left our office and walked down to see Luke. My heart beat as fast as a woodpecker's tap, but I was never more resolved in my life to complete this task.

At the sound of my knock, he looked up with a little bit of weariness on his face.

"Can I talk to you for a few minutes, Luke?"

"Sure. Come on in." He pushed the papers he had been perusing over to one side of his desk.

"Luke," I said. "This is private and I need to close the door."

Luke nodded, and I closed the door behind me before sitting down in one of his guest chairs. His office was small, appropriate for a front-line manager to talk to no more than two people at a time. I had been in there several times, but never for a personal problem.

"Luke." I paused and took a breath. "Luke, my marriage is not going to work. My husband is abusive, and I need to leave him." There. The first part of my message was out.

Luke dropped his head down quickly. I knew he was thinking back to the time when we were talking in his office, and he suddenly asked me if that was a bruise on my cheek. This was after I'd taken a few days off work after Mark hit me during lunchtime. I had answered "yes," and then I quickly jumped back into the discussion topic.

Now he raised his head up and said sincerely, "I'm sorry."

"No. It's my fault for not recognizing what I was getting into. He hit me while we were dating. I should have broken up with him then instead of marrying him. But it's done now."

"What are you going to do?"

"I'm going back to Columbus. I seriously doubt that my

husband will leave me alone if I stay here. I need to leave this weekend. I need to resign my job today."

Luke fell back in his chair. "Oh, I'm really sorry to hear that, Maria. Can't you just leave the marriage and move in with one of your friends?"

"I wish it were that easy, but he is insanely jealous. He would just take that as a sign that I'm trying to see someone else. The best thing for me to do is to get away from him entirely. Some place where he cannot get to me."

"You don't think he would follow you to Columbus?"

"No. He is not a good money manager, so he would have to take his paycheck as soon as he got it and buy a plane ticket to Columbus in order to follow me."

"How do you plan to get away from him? Is there anything that I can help you with?"

"No. This is something that I have to do by myself and, at this point, I have no idea how I'm going to get away. I just know that I need to do it, and I need to do it quickly."

Luke shook his head a little as if to clear it. "OK, well, let me get the paperwork together, and we'll get all this finished today."

"Thank you, Luke."

I got up to leave.

"Oh," I turned back to his desk. "I'd like to keep this quiet. I don't want anyone to know what I'm doing."

"Well, you know they will all know on Monday what has happened."

"Monday is okay. I just don't want to talk about it or chance someone saying something to him today."

"I understand." Luke paused, and then said, "One more thing, Maria."

"Yes?"

"If you ever decide that you can come back to Atlanta to live, will you come back here and work for us?"

I gave a slight smile, glad for the verification that he had been happy with my work. "Yes, I will."

"I'm really sorry about this, Maria. You know, marriages that are made in heaven are wonderful, but those that are made in hell are just that—they are in hell."

I nodded.

He stood up and followed me out of the office. I turned left down the hall, and he headed right, toward the department head's office.

By the time I got back to my office, Cathy was smiling up at me and telling me that Mark had called.

I walked back to the desk where our only office phone sat and called him back. I was hoping that none of my other six co-workers could tell that I was shaking. Mark called me every day at work, but this time I was scared that somehow he knew what I was planning.

"Maria, I'm sorry," he said when he answered the phone. "They called a lunchtime meeting for all the consultants, so I won't be able to pick you up for lunch."

"Oh. It's not a problem. I can get something from the vending machines."

"OK. I'll see you after work."

He did not know that this was a big load off my shoulders. I really didn't want to be with Mark when I was in the middle of making plans to leave him.

Chapter 10

BALL OF CONFUSION

WHEN I LEFT THE OFFICE that evening, Steve and Cathy wished me a good weekend as they left. I sent the wish back to them but, inwardly, I wondered what kind of weekend I would be having. I still didn't know how I was going to get away; all I knew was that I wasn't coming back to the office on Monday.

Mark sat in the car, outside the building, waiting for me as usual. I smiled at him, trying hard not to give off any impression of what was really on my mind.

He was caught up in another event anyway. "I had to counsel one of the teenage boys today. His mother brought him in because he was caught slipping into one of the vacant units."

"What was he doing in the vacant unit?" I asked.

"He was working with some older boys who were stealing the appliances. He was smaller, so he could get through the windows. Then he would open the front door and let the thieves come in."

"Who caught him?"

"A neighbor saw him going through the window, and the neighbor knew his mother. So instead of calling the police, he yelled at the boy, and then he called his mother."

"Hm. Did that really help the situation?"

"Well, the boy ran. I assume the thieves left, too, after he never opened the door."

"What did you say to him?"

I really wanted Mark to do most of the talking so that I could just nod my head and say "Uh-huh." Fortunately, Mark's pride about his talk with the young man made him launch into a long oration about their conversation. All I had to do was pretend that I was listening.

We were entering our apartment as Mark said. "I really think I got through to him by the time he and his mother left."

"Good job!" I responded, happy that now I could busy myself with dinner while Mark took the dogs out. After that, he typically retreated to the bedroom to watch TV and unwind.

I used this alone time to ponder how I could get away. I never went anywhere in the car alone—I never even drove the car anymore—so there was really no opportunity for me to leave that way. If I just told Mark I was leaving, that would call for a vicious fight. I went to bed that night with no plausible ideas for escape.

Mark stayed in the house all day Saturday; then, finally, as the sun was setting, he patted the car keys in his pocket and said, "I'm heading out. I'll be back in a bit."

As usual, he didn't tell me how long he was going to be out. I figured he didn't want to give me any time to carry out an imaginary "rendezvous" with someone else. I trusted him to play chess for hours with friends or to just hang out and talk, but he could not return the trust.

After he left, I started watching a movie on TV. The dogs had come in the bedroom and settled themselves beside my chair. I stroked them, while I continued to think about my options for a nonviolent exit. I really hated to leave Leta and Hasana. This statuesque duo had been attentive and loving companions, but I had to get away from Mark.

It was odd remembering how Mark said he had spotted Leta as a malnourished, neglected puppy in the pound. He had literally saved her life by nursing her back to health afterwards. Now, here I was, needing to flee from Mark so that I could save *my* life.

Although I knew Mark loved his dogs, I had never liked the way he disciplined them. On the few times when they messed up, he would grab them by the front of their necks with one hand and raise them up from the floor. Then with the other hand open, he'd land one hard slap on the side of their faces. The first time I saw that, I wanted to ask why he didn't use a rolled-up newspaper on their backsides instead, but he was their owner, and they were devoted to him. So I just walked away whenever I knew he was about to discipline them.

I really wished I could run away with them, but they were not my dogs and that would be stealing. I continued thinking about how I was going to leave Mark and the dogs. He had been gone about an hour when the phone rang.

"Hello?"

It was Mark. "What are you doing?" he asked.

"Just watching this movie on TV."

"No, you're not. You've got somebody in there with you."

"Mark, I do not have anybody in the house. I am here with the dogs and I am watching TV."

"I'm coming back there to find out!"

He hung up the phone. My heart was throbbing in my ears. I sensed a beating on the horizon.

I decided on the spot that I would go to the airport and take a plane back to Columbus that night. I needed to get a cab since Mark was in my car, but I could not wait at the apartment for the cab to arrive.

I picked up my purse and looked for a heavy jacket. Airline

travelers didn't dress casually in the 70s. I was wearing dark brown bell bottom pants with a yellow knitted top, and there was no time to change. I hurriedly found the matching jacket to my pants and added a pair of tan heels to create a suitable business-like appearance for a Saturday night.

Very quickly, I scribbled a note saying "I am totally innocent of all these thoughts you have about me. I cannot live like this anymore". I left the note on the bed and ran to the living room which had the clearest view of the parking lot.

It was nighttime, but I had to make sure Mark was not already in the parking lot. Cautiously, I peeked out from the heavy living room curtains, scanning the area under the low glow of the complex's lampposts. Then I led the dogs into the front closet, where they stayed whenever we were out. Afterwards, I dashed out of the apartment.

A convenience store stood across the street from the complex. I could call a cab from there, but I had to get through the complex without Mark spotting me as he drove back in. Fortunately, the moonless night sky provided me with a good, dark cover.

I left through the back exit of our building so that I wouldn't be exposed in the parking lot. Running through the grass, my heels caught in the ground with each step I took in the dark. I thought of how this was the area where Mark took the dogs out several times a day. I sniffed and prayed that I wouldn't step into any dog mess.

I crossed the two-lane main street of our apartment complex, finally out of the grassy areas. But, again, I needed to stay off the roads that the cars took. That's when I ran behind the apartment buildings on that side of the main street. Some windows glowed with bright lights, while other windows were as black as the night. I was a lone, dark shadow running behind those apartments in the night. I knew that if anyone saw me flying by their windows, they would be extremely suspicious of my intentions.

I needed to get by those apartments as fast as possible, so I tried running a little more quickly, until I made it to Camp Creek Parkway, the main road leading to the freeway. Once there, I stopped. I hadn't realized how winded I had become.

While I hung back in the shadows of the trees on the parkway, I worked to slow my breathing. I didn't dare run across the parkway while car headlights were coming my way. One of those cars might have been mine.

When the break in traffic finally came, I sprinted across the street. The asphalt gave me much more freedom to run than the grass had allowed. My eyes scanned the length of the parking lot to make sure my Firebird wasn't there, before I rushed into the brightly lit store.

There was only a moment in which I could let my eyes adjust to the difference in light.

"Where is your pay phone?" I breathlessly asked the store clerk. He pointed to the phone in the back corner, and I went over to pick up the yellow pages so that I could find the number for a cab.

After making the short call, it was waiting time. *Should I buy something?* I wondered. *No, I don't have that much money, and I really can't be in the front of the store where the cash register and windows are.*

I hid in the bathroom for 10 minutes, then cautiously emerged and looked at each person moving about the store. No Mark, thank goodness.

I remained in the back of the store, away from the windows, hoping that the cab would get there soon. A man came through the door of the store. Another older man left through the door. Every movement made my heart jump, even though the constant movement meant that the clerk probably didn't have time to worry about me.

The cash register dinged constantly, as it kept ringing up sales. The voices of various conversations rose and fell.

I watched each person, knowing I looked suspicious—a young

black woman lingering between the aisles of the convenience store and not buying anything. But my only other choice was to try to find a dark spot to stand just outside the store, and I thought that might look even more suspicious.

I prayed earnestly that Mark would not stop in this store tonight. There were no dark shadows inside for me to hide in, and there were only three or four short aisles of inventory.

After a half-hour wait, the cab pulled up in front of the store. I moved closer to the door, checked the parking lot again with my eyes, then walked very quickly to the cab.

Sinking down into the darkened back seat, I told the driver where I wanted to go and let out a long, deep breath. I was still in danger, but at least I was getting farther away from Mark.

I had been hoping that the $10 bill in my purse would be enough to pay for the trip to the airport. If the meter rang up $9.50 before I reached the airport, I had decided to ask the cabbie to let me out so that I could walk the rest of the way to the airport.

Fortunately, I managed to make it all the way to the airport for $8.70—$1.30 left and almost 500 more miles to go.

Chapter 11

KEEP ON PUSHING

INSIDE THE AIRPORT, THE COVER of darkness retreated as I was now awash in the glaring white lights of the terminal. I hurried up to a dark-haired man at the Delta ticket stand and said, "I want to catch the next plane going north. I just need a one-way ticket."

"Where do you want to go?"

"Anywhere North," I repeated, emphasizing the last word.

He pushed his black-rimmed glasses back up his nose. "Well, if you tell me exactly where you want to end up, I can probably get you close." The man was just trying to be helpful, but I didn't need his help for anything except to get me out of Atlanta quickly.

Exasperated, I said, "I'm going to Columbus, Ohio, but I want to leave here as quickly as possible. Just put me on *any* plane headed north!"

The agent looked down at his computer terminal and typed something. He watched the response that clacked back out, and then said, "I have a plane leaving here in two hours, going to Cincinnati. From there, you can transfer to a flight to Columbus."

"I can't wait two hours. Do you have something going north earlier than that?"

"I have a flight leaving for Baltimore in about 90 minutes,

but that's not much different than waiting the two hours. And the Cincinnati flight would get you closer to your destination."

At my frown, he continued his argument. "It wouldn't cost you nearly as much as going through Baltimore and then doubling back to Columbus. Plus, I can book you all the way through, since there will be a flight leaving Cincinnati for Columbus not long after you get there."

The agent's blue eyes widened, and his head tilted slightly as if to ask, "What do you think?"

I sighed. "OK. I guess I'll take that." I looked back at the airport doors, just to make sure that Mark wasn't coming in. There was a good chance he would figure out where I had gone, but I didn't know how soon he would come to that conclusion.

I had already determined that I could use my charge card if the fare wasn't too expensive. The charge card payment had been two months overdue, since Mark had borrowed money from me to pay a couple of lingering bills. Fortunately, I recently paid the past due amounts on the card, so I knew I could still use it.

Please, Lord, let me have enough money left on that card to pay for this.

The man told me the cost of the fare, and I nodded. I handed him my charge card which was approved for the price of the ticket.

The man's fingers tapped on his terminal, while relief swelled deep within me. I wouldn't let that feeling show on my face because I didn't want the man to know that I hadn't been sure I could pay for the ticket.

"OK, Miss Jordan. Just give me a minute and I will have your ticket all ready to go. I am booking you all the way to Columbus. Your flight will arrive there at 11:52 p.m."

He pecked on the terminal a few more times.

"Any bags to check?" He raised his eyebrows at me.

"No. No bags."

The ticket agent pointed me to the gate where my flight would be in two hours. Now I had to wait and pray. This was years before airport restrictions had gotten so tight that you had to have a ticket in order to get into the boarding area, so I was worried that Mark would show up at some point before I got on my plane.

First, though, I needed to call home. I walked down the long terminal hall. I kept walking past the gate where my plane would board. When I found a secluded area of pay phones, I picked up a phone and asked the operator to put through a collect call to the phone in my old bedroom. This was an extra phone line that I had gotten after I started working summer jobs. My father spent long hours on the main phone line, talking to church members and other preachers. It was almost impossible for the rest of the family to get a call in or out. After I left Columbus, my mother and brother had gotten used to having another phone, so they kept that line.

My mother answered the phone and agreed to pay for the call.

"Well, hello, Maria! I'm surprised you called on this line." Unlike the main home line, this line had no extensions. I always called home on the main number so that all my family could pick up the extensions and talk to me at the same time. Today, I only wanted to speak to one person—my mother.

"Yeah, Mama. I need to tell you something."

"OK."

Without mincing words, I said, "Mark tried to choke me the other night."

"What?!?" She was surprised, but I kept talking.

"I got a call from work about a program that wasn't working, and he accused me of having an affair with the computer operator who called me. Then he grabbed me around the neck and started choking me."

"Umph. You walked into that with no warning!"

"Well …. no, not quite."

My mother didn't say anything, so I went on.

I told her about the first slap and waited to see if she had a comment, but she didn't.

I described the second incident. Still my mother said nothing.

"But then I talked to the minister of the church we had been attending, and she advised me that we just needed to get married. I thought that would take care of the jealousy problem. But then this happened."

I stopped talking. My mother's silent disappointment in my choices spoke loudly over the phone. We had had a conversation quite some years before, where she told me that a man once hit her and, although she was a mild-mannered person, she said she picked up a chair and tried to kill him with it.

Mama had said that I should never let a man hit me. Now I was saying that I not only let him hit me, but I also married him afterwards. She didn't lecture me. In fact, she still hadn't said anything.

I finally blurted out, "Aren't you going to tell me to leave him?"

"No," she said. "No. You have to decide for yourself what you're going to do because you alone will have to *live with* that decision. Nobody else can make that decision for you."

That was not the answer I was expecting.

She went on. "If I tell you to leave him and you later decide you're unhappy and want to go back to him, then you would be upset with me….probably just like you're upset now with the minister who advised you to marry him."

I shook my head vigorously, even though she couldn't see me.

"Well, I am leaving him," I said. "I'm at the airport now, and I've bought a ticket to come back home. I didn't pack anything. I just left. I am not---"

I stopped mid-sentence because I heard the confident click-clack of Mark's shoes coming around the corner of the secluded, but well-lit spot I'd found. Everything stood still as I held my breath, waiting for the confrontation.

When the clacking shoes got around to me, I saw that it was a middle-aged white man who kept going right past me. I slowly let out my breath again.

"I thought that was Mark coming around the corner, but it wasn't," I told my mother. "I'm coming home! My plane should arrive at 11:52 p.m."

"OK," she said gravely. "I'll be at the airport to pick you up. I'll be praying for you."

I hung up the phone and looked at the giant clock on the wall. There was at least another hour before boarding time. I was far beyond my gate, but I knew I didn't want to be too far away from other people. If Mark came to the airport and found me, I wanted to be where, hopefully, somebody would call security if he started hitting me or dragging me away.

I walked to another gate where about 30 people were waiting. I looked at the board over the ticket agent area and saw that their plane would leave in 40 minutes. That was almost the same amount of time that I had before boarding my plane.

I debated whether I should be facing the direction that Mark would come in, or facing the opposite direction so that it would harder for him to see me. I finally decided that I needed to be on the lookout for trouble, rather than be surprised by it. I sat down and anxiously watched and waited.

Periodically, I looked at the people around me. Most people had family members there to lovingly send them off. Most of them were probably headed somewhere for an enjoyable vacation or to be with other family members. Only a few were alone. I doubted that any of them were in fear for their lives.

I knew my mother was earnestly praying for me in Columbus. I also knew that she was well aware of how much danger I was in if Mark caught up with me at the airport. For a minute, I wondered if she told my father what was going on, or was she going to wait to see if I went through with my plan to leave Atlanta?

I remembered that once a friend asked me what it was like to have a mother who never yelled at you. I had to stop and consider the question because I never realized that she didn't holler. Although she didn't spare the rod when I was a child, when I was a teenager and young adult she spent more time listening to me and asking questions that required me to think about my actions.

Once another boyfriend had gone to Japan for a temporary tour of duty with the Air Force after we had only dated for a couple of months. Like Mark, he was 10 years older than me, while his close friends were nearer my age. Among the many letters we wrote back and forth was one in which he asked me to marry him.

I told my mother about the proposal and said that I was seriously considering saying "Yes." Her only comment was, "You know, you really need to date someone for over a year to make sure you really know them. People can hide their personalities for a while, but very few can hide their true selves for more than a year."

"Well, we've been dating for four months now, and he is just the sweetest person."

She smiled slightly. "When I say 'dating,' I'm talking about being around a person—seeing them, going places with them, interacting with them and your friends. Not just writing letters to them."

Needless to say, that relationship died on its own, but was Mark the exception to Mom's dating guideline? I had dated Mark for over a year. No! I stopped to calculate the number of months. It was exactly one year, almost to the day, when Mark first slapped me. Mom had been right again, and I had been too in love and too deep in the relationship to want to pull myself out.

Well, now I was going to do something about it. I continued to watch everyone who came down the terminal hallway, but nobody resembling Mark appeared.

The agents called for the first boarders on the plane, and I watched as a few people went forward with their tickets.

They called for the next group of boarders. More people went forward to get in line for boarding. The families who weren't traveling started moving away, as more and more travelers went through the gate and up the ramp to the plane.

Eventually, the gate area was empty, except for me and the two ticket agents. They both looked over at me questioningly. I bit my lip and rose from my seat. It was time for me to go to my gate. I guessed that they would start boarding there in about 20 minutes.

I walked away. Slowly.

A restroom! I quickly slipped inside to kill time. I had no idea if Mark would be waiting for me at my departure gate. I went inside a toilet stall.

I was slow and deliberate about everything I did.

Washing my hands with the liquid soap.

Pulling down the paper towel from the dispenser.

Drying my hands until they felt rough.

Checking my makeup. I had brought none with me, so there really was nothing I could do about it. I pulled the Afro pick out of my purse.

Picking and patting my hair.

I leaned on the sink with both hands and looked down at the drain.

Lord, will somebody keep him from beating me if it comes to that? Or will people just look at us and keep walking?

I smoothed my jacket and pants, hung my purse on my shoulder, and walked out of the bathroom.

Now it was my turn to click and clack down the hallway, but my pace was a lot slower than usual.

I saw a water fountain. *Yes! Get some water for my parched throat!*

As I rose up from my long, cool drink at the fountain, I wondered, *How can everything around me look so normal tonight? People are traveling, some are smiling, and some are distracted. The airport PA is announcing arrivals and departures. It is business as usual for the rest of the world.*

Nobody there knew the trouble I was in—nobody, except God.

I had almost reached my departure gate, but I decided to slow down and scan the crowd.

No Mark.

I checked in with the ticket agents who were at the departure gate.

Again, I sat and faced the part of the hallway where all folks coming toward this gate would have to travel.

This 15-minute wait seemed so much longer than the 40-minute wait at the other gate. But, finally, they called the first-class passengers who seemed unusually slow about getting on. There was a pause. Then they called the rest of the passengers, and I moved quickly to get in line.

As I stood there behind a woman and her toddler, I refused to look back. At every moment, I expected to feel a heavy hand on my shoulder.

Finally, I was moving up the ramp. *I had almost made it!*

I got on board and made my way past the pilots, past the stewardesses, and on to find my seat number. I was next to a thin, young man who had already put a pillow behind his head.

Good! I really don't want to talk either!

Cautiously, I sat down, felt for the seat belt, and secured it.

Others got on board behind me. I looked at each person, fully expecting to see Mark come through—even without a ticket.

It appeared that the stream of passengers was over, but we still we didn't take off.

The airline stewardesses were busy with their tasks. They came through and made sure we were all comfortable. I would not be comfortable until we were in the air, but I didn't say that.

I kept waiting and watching the aisle. Another late passenger came in and walked down the aisle past me. More minutes passed.

Finally, I felt a slight jerk of the plane, and I saw the stewardesses taking their positions to give us their instructions.

I had really made it! I thought with great relief. *I was getting away from Mark.*

Chapter 12

THIN LINE BETWEEN LOVE AND HATE

My eyes skimmed the crowd that was standing around the arrival gate in the Columbus airport. I was interested only in seeing a tall, tan, woman, looking much younger than her real age of 47. And there she was, just on the edge of the crowd. My mother.

After giving me a big hug, she held me by the shoulders so that she could look at me, relief all over her face.

Her expression became serious as she delivered some news. "Mark called the house."

"What? When did that happen?"

"It was about an hour after you called me."

"What did he say?"

"He was very cool and calm. He said he wanted me to know that you were coming in on the 11:52 p.m. flight from Cincinnati. He also wanted you to call him when you got in."

We had begun walking toward the exit of the airport.

"So he tried to act like it was nothing special, huh?" I said.

"Yeah. I played along with his act. I didn't tell him that I'd already talked to you."

"Did you tell Dad what was happening?"

"Not really. After Mark called, I told Dad that he called and said you were flying in tonight."

"Didn't he want to know why?"

"Sure. I told him I'd let you explain it when you got in."

"I've been thinking about that explanation ever since the plane finally got off the ground in Atlanta."

"Well, the important thing is that you are safe," my mother said. "Once I got that call from Mark, I was still praying, but at least I knew he wasn't going to come to the airport after you. I wish I could have let you know that, but there was no way to contact you."

"Yeah, I would really like to have known that. I was scared the whole time I was in the Atlanta airport."

We headed through the dark parking lot. My jacket, which had been quite adequate in Atlanta, was barely keeping the Ohio chill off me. I pulled it tighter around me.

"What are you planning to do about clothes?" My mother looked down at the heels I was wearing.

"I don't know. At some point I need to get back down there to get my stuff. I was thinking that I still had some money left on my clothing store accounts here. Maybe I can get a couple of outfits to tide me over."

I always had big feet, so I could not buy shoes at regular stores. Although I wore heels every day to work, I didn't walk around the house in heels. There were still lots of things to figure out. My car was in Atlanta. I needed to get back there soon and retrieve it. I had my bedroom suite in storage. I still had bills I had to pay. I had no job.

We made it to the car, and my whole body began to relax as my mother drove me home. There was too much to figure out. Tonight, I just needed to let my family know what was going on and get a good night's sleep. It had been a very tough three days and, for the first time in several hours, I was able to lean my head back and take a deep breath.

When we walked in the side door of the house after midnight, my bespectacled father was sitting in the kitchen in his robe and pajamas. I imagined that my brother had long since been in the bed.

"Hello, Dad." I walked over and kissed him on the cheek.

"Hello." He looked up at me, solemnly and obviously concerned about what was causing this sudden visit. "Here. Have a seat. Let's talk."

He reached for the handle of the refrigerator behind him. "You hungry? I fried some drumsticks. We can heat up some other food to go with it." He had always been the best cook of the family. He made sure to end his activities every weekday so that he could get home early and cook dinner before the rest of us made it back.

"Not really. I'm just worn out."

"Yeah? Well, tell me what's going on so we can all get some rest." He set his glasses on the table and looked at me expectantly.

I sat down at the table and told the whole story to both my parents. Periodically, my father would shake his head a little, or say "Hmph," or look over at my mother to see her reaction. But generally he was calm.

Somewhere in the middle of my story, I realized that, as a pastor, he had probably heard similar stories from others once or twice. It just had never been about his daughter and her husband.

I ended by saying, "I don't know what to do about all my things I left behind. I will think about that some more after I get some rest."

"Yeah. Well, we all need to get some rest. Thank the Lord you made it safe and sound."

It was after 1 a.m. by then. The next day was Sunday, which was always a busy day in our household.

"Oh, yeah. I need to return Mark's call before I go to sleep."

My father lightly put his hand on my arm and said, "You can wait until tomorrow."

"If I do, he'll just call back tonight and keep calling back until I answer. He knows what time the plane got in."

"Hm. He's your husband," he said. "You know what to do."

I went into the bedroom and shut the door. My mother had given me one of her nightgowns, so I laid it on the bed before dialing Mark's number. Nothing had been changed about the room since I left town. I had decorated it with dark purple curtains and bedspread. I even had made a matching dark purple skirt for my dressing table. Now all that dark taffeta reflected my somber mood.

The phone only rang once before Mark picked up.

"Hello."

My voice was straight business. "Hello, Mark. You wanted me to call you when I got to Columbus."

"Yeah. How was your flight?"

I rolled my eyes up toward the ceiling. "It was fine. How did you know that I had caught a flight home?"

"I finally figured out that you might have chosen that option. I just didn't know you would book a flight using your maiden name, instead of your married name."

"My charge card is still in my maiden name."

"Oh, that was it."

"Yes. I'm tired, so I need to go."

"OK. I just wanted to tell you that I was wrong, and I apologize for making our marriage stressful. I know that you are a good woman. Go ahead and spend some time there with your grandmother. When you've had enough time, come on back and you'll see that I'm a man who appreciates what I've been blessed with."

"Mark, I'm not coming back. I did not come here to visit my grandmother. I came here because I am leaving you."

"We can talk about that a little later."

"I am not coming back! And I am very tired, so I'm going to hang up now."

"OK. Sleep well and I'll talk to you tomorrow."

"Mark, I have nothing further to say to you. You do not need to call me tomorrow."

"Have a good night's rest, Maria."

I hung up the phone. I couldn't believe that he was acting as if this were a minor issue and that I was just home to visit my grandmother. I was extremely angry at Mark as I got ready for bed. But I was also very tired, so I worked at not thinking about anything, except that I was safely away from him. I quickly fell asleep.

Chapter 13

EXPRESS YOURSELF

My brother, Richard, was a six-foot-six, handsome college freshman who lived at home while attending Ohio Dominican College in Columbus. When he saw me coming out of my room the next morning, he yelled my name in surprise. Everybody, except me, was getting ready for church, so I quickly hugged him and explained that Mark and I were having problems in our marriage and that I had left him.

"Where is your car? How did you get here?" he asked when he looked out the window to the driveway.

"I left in a hurry. I'll have to go back and get the car."

I was busy trying to wash and dry an orange dress that I had accidentally left behind during one of my prior trips home. My plan was to go to afternoon church service, until it dawned on me that my brother might share my troubles with his girlfriend or other church members. I stopped him before he left the house.

"Do not tell anyone else that I am back," I said emphatically. "I'm not ready to answer questions. They will eventually know that I'm here, and they will eventually figure out that I've left my husband. Okay?"

"Okay."

I took time to rest and prepare dinner while everyone was at church. That afternoon, while we dined on fried pork chops, macaroni, and carrots, my phone started ringing and I ignored it.

There was an afternoon church service to go to so, with my one outfit now clean, I headed out of the house with my family. A couple of church members expressed surprise that I was back in Columbus alone, since they knew that I had recently gotten married. I just nodded, raised my eyebrows, and smiled.

After the afternoon service, my mother drove me to the nursing home to see my grandmother.

"How is Muz doing?" I asked during the short ride.

"Not well. She's in a lot of pain. There are a lot of decisions to be made. Boon-Boon tends to look to me for making the decisions. They have been married a long time, and this is tearing him up."

"Yeah, I'm sure. But she's your mother. How are you doing?"

Mama gave me a quick, weary smile and a sigh. "I'm hanging in there."

She pulled up into the parking lot of the nursing home, turned off the car, sat back, and asked, "And what about you?"

"Oh, I don't know. I cannot believe all this is happening."

"I'm sure," she agreed. "Why did you marry him?"

"I loved him. I *still* love him. He can be very sweet and caring and kind. We have good times together, just doing the simplest things. I thought he was the man for me."

"You didn't think that he would hit you again after the first time?"

"No, I didn't. I'd never had a boyfriend hit me before. Dad never hit you. I knew that had to be a one-time mistake."

"Now tell me about the second time. You said a minister told you that you two needed to get married?" she asked incredulously.

"Yeah!" I looked at her like I couldn't believe it either. "I think—I think that Mark called her and convinced her that he wasn't that kind of person."

"Why do you think that?"

"Well, I told him I was going to call her after he hit me. By the time I looked up the number, her line was busy. I didn't realize it then, but now I figure that Mark called her and told her something like he just wanted us to get married, and then he wouldn't be jealous anymore."

"Didn't you think then that it was rather strange advice?"

"I was surprised at first. But then, I mean—do you remember Sammy?"

"Yeah. He was the soldier that you started seeing the summer before you went away to Fisk, right?"

"Yes. Well, I was really jealous of him. I didn't want him to talk to anybody else, or dance with anybody else at parties, or look at anybody else. That jealousy felt like a wave of fire taking over my body!"

"Really?"

"Really! I just made his life miserable when he was out with me. And I made everybody else around us uncomfortable. They could see my anger in the way I folded my arms and frowned at whoever he was talking to. I didn't like creating that kind of atmosphere, but that's what I did."

"I had no idea. Did you ever try to hit him?"

"No," I scoffed. "I fussed at him anytime that I suspected he was paying attention to somebody else."

"Why did you feel that way?"

"I don't know. Well, yes, I do know. The previous boyfriend—the only 'boyfriend' I had before. You remember Ralph, the one who dropped me for Candace, don't you?"

"Yes."

"Well, I think after that, I was insecure about my friends being around my boyfriend. I think that's what made me so jealous with Sammy."

"How did you resolve that?"

"Um. That's interesting." I searched my mind for an answer.

"I don't really know," I finally said. "When I left town and went to Fisk, I dated other guys—I even *liked* a couple of them a lot—even though I was crazy about Sammy. Maybe I saw that you didn't really have to be jealous if the other person loved you."

I frowned because I couldn't figure it out. "I don't know....I was not near as jealous when I came back for summer break.... and then we eventually broke up…and then, I was never jealous of anybody else after that. It's strange. I can't tell you exactly what made me get past that."

"So? Is that why you had some sympathy for Mark's jealousy?"

"Yes! I really thought that he would eventually see that there was no reason to be jealous … that he would realize I was not going to leave him for somebody else, or even flirt with somebody else. And maybe marriage would be the way for him to come to that realization."

"Well, too bad he couldn't get around to seeing that."

She was silent for just a few seconds before she went on, "You know, something interesting happened with Muz this week."

"What was that?"

"She was in one of her pain-free moments, and she suddenly got real upset. She was looking off in the distance, and she started saying, 'Maria can't breathe! She can't breathe!'"

I frowned, "Why was she saying that?"

"It was almost like she was psychic, but I didn't realize it at the time. It was either just before or on the very day when you said Mark choked you."

"Really?"

"Yeah. I mean, I know she isn't psychic—I don't believe in that kind of stuff. But the timing of that was strange. She hasn't said anything about it since then, and the whole episode only lasted a minute or less, but it's just really strange."

"Yeah, my goodness. That is strange."

She gave a quick pat to my knee. "It's getting late. Come on, we'd better get inside to see Muz."

The frosty Ohio winds were blowing when we got out of the car. In contrast, the still, bold smell of urine greeted us as we entered the front door of the nursing home. Mama led me to the room where Muz was. Like my mother, Muz usually had a smile on her face; this time, though, she didn't. Her arms and legs had become very thin, and her skin hung loosely around her limbs. There was weariness in her eyes. I smiled at her.

"Ree-bee," she greeted me weakly, still without a smile. My mother immediately attended to the things that my grandmother wanted—another sheet on the bed, a cool washcloth on her head.

Soon Muz was able to get a few moments of sleep. We left when it seemed like she was getting longer stretches of restful sleep.

That was when I remembered I had another problem in Atlanta.

Chapter 14

"LET'S STAY TOGETHER"

My cousin Kirk was being released on parole the very next day, and I had previously agreed to pick him up at the Pen. With Mark's attack and my decision to leave him, I had forgotten all about Kirk. I needed some way to let him know that I would not be there. I called long-distance to the prison, knowing that I could not initiate a call to a prisoner. However, since he was being released the next day, I hoped they would let me leave a message.

The prison staff refused to take a message, even though I explained the situation to them. I had visions of Kirk standing there on this jubilant occasion, being thoroughly disappointed because his ride to the bus station was nowhere in sight. But there was nothing more I could do.

As soon as I got off the phone with the Atlanta Pen, my phone rang. I figured it would be Mark again, and I was right.

"Hello, Maria, and how was your day?"

"It was fine," I said flatly.

"Good. Mine went fairly well. I went to church, and Rev. Moore asked about you."

"What did you tell her?"

"I told her you were in Columbus visiting your sick grandmother."

"That's not why I'm in Columbus."

"No?"

"That's not the reason why I left Atlanta."

"But you *are* visiting your grandmother, and she is sick."

"Yeah, but you might as well tell the truth about it. I'm not coming back."

"You are my wife. I am your husband. We love each other. We belong together. But I should have suggested that you go see your grandmother before now."

"Mark, that has nothing to do with it! You tried to strangle me. You keep accusing me of doing things that I would not even dream of doing. That is no way for a husband to treat his wife."

"You are absolutely right. I let my emotions get away with me. I promise you *I won't do that again.*"

"I know you won't do it again, because I won't be there for you to do it to me again."

"Have you stopped loving me?"

I thought about that question for a few seconds.

"I love you. You are my husband. But we cannot live together—"

"We can live together. All it takes is for two people to love each other through their faults. Don't you believe that love conquers all?"

"No, Mark. I don't think love can conquer this. You have no control over your actions. It's been, what? Three times that you have attacked me! If you loved me, you wouldn't have done it the first time. No, we've tried it. It didn't work. End of story."

"I love you, Maria. I love you with all my heart. I've messed up but, please, give me another chance. I won't fail you again."

"Mark, this is really wearing me out. I've had a long day, and I need to get some rest. You don't need to ask me to come back. I am not doing it."

"What are you going to do about your job? They'll be expecting you to come into the office tomorrow."

"Let me worry about that."

"Maria—"

"Mark, I'm hanging up now."

"OK. I'll give you all the space and time you need."

"What do you—?" There was no need to keep talking. Mark was impossible. I wanted him to leave me alone. That was the space I needed.

He finished the conversation. "Good night, and I'll talk to you later."

I hung up the phone. I didn't want to talk to him later. Everything was at a failing point now. I felt as if I wasn't able to follow through on any of my commitments—my marriage or getting a message to my cousin on what should have been a happy day for him.

I laid my head down on my bed and closed my eyes.

The next morning I woke up knowing that it was time to pick up the pieces of my life and move forward. I had no clothes, and I had no job. I had three clothing store charge cards in Columbus and, fortunately, I had recently paid my bills on all of them. I had a little money left on each card, just enough to buy one or two outfits. I borrowed my father's car and spent part of the day buying new outfits that I could wear to interviews and to church.

That night Mark called.

"I called your office this morning and told them that you weren't coming in because you had gone to Columbus to visit your sick grandmother."

"Mark, would you quit telling that lie to people?"

"I had to tell them something."

"I told you to let me worry about my job."

"Well, there was something you didn't know."

"What?"

"They had planned a surprise lunch for you today. I was supposed to get you to the lunch without you knowing what was going on. They had bought some wedding gifts for us. After you left town, I had to let them know that the lunch was off so they could cancel the reservations at the restaurant in time."

I was quiet as this all sank into my mind. I didn't have a clue that my co-workers were planning anything for me. I was sure that everybody would find out that I had quit my job and left my new husband that Monday morning. I hadn't cared what they thought or said at that point, since I would not see any of them anymore.

Now I wondered what they must have thought when Mark called and said that I was just away visiting my grandmother. The whole circle of events was making Mark look like somewhat of a clueless idiot.

"Mark," I said sadly. "I handed in my resignation on Friday. My manager already knew that I wasn't coming back. I'm sure he told everybody else this morning."

Mark went silent for a whole minute. My heart was aching for his embarrassment.

"Humph." He finally said. "You really got me on that one."

That was the last comment before he ended the conversation.

Chapter 15

"GOT TO GET YOU INTO MY LIFE"

THE NEXT EVENING, MY MOTHER and I were in the kitchen alone, cleaning up after dinner. I told her that I had found some interview clothes, and I brought them out on hangers to show them to her.

"I hear your phone ringing from time to time," she said. "Since you don't call me or Richard, I figure it's Mark still calling for you."

"Yeah. You won't believe what happened yesterday!" I went on to tell her about the surprise lunch/shower.

"That was nice that your co-workers wanted to do that for you. I can understand Mark not wanting to tell them that you had left him already."
"Yeah. I felt kind of sorry for him, but not really because it's his fault that this is happening."

We went on to talk about job possibilities. I was concerned about what I should put on job applications for the reason why I left my last job.

"You can just put 'Personal Reasons.' You don't have to explain what they are," my mother said as she dried some silverware.

"Really?"

Mama was a supervisor in a government agency, so I trusted her judgment on these matters. I was about to ask if she had ever gotten resumes with that reason stated, but my phone was ringing again.

I walked into my room and answered it. It was Mark with the same circular conversation, just like a needle stuck in the groove of a scratched vinyl record. My mind was only on what my next steps should be. I ended that call as soon as I could.

I decided that the most important thing right now was for me to find a job. I started scouring the help wanted ads in the newspaper for computer programming jobs. After my work in Atlanta, I now knew another programming language. This made me even more marketable, since most programmers at that time only had job experience in one language.

On Wednesday, I arranged for an interview with one of the companies who were advertising for somebody with my skills.

Mark called that night.

"How is your grandmother?" he asked pleasantly.

"She's in a lot of pain, but she is able to hold a conversation when the pain is not hitting."

"What are the doctors saying?"

"I haven't talked to them but, according to my mother, the doctors said it was just a matter of time. It's hard to watch."

"I can imagine. How was your day otherwise?"

"Well, I've been busy calling people in response to help wanted ads in the newspaper."

"Why are you doing that?"

"You don't need to ask."

"Maria," he sighed briefly. "We can make this work. I will never, ever hit you again. I know what I did was wrong. I see how much it affected you. I am so, so sorry for hurting you. Come on back and let's make this work!"

"Mark, I am not coming back. The hitting and choking is not

something that you have control over. You will never get past it until you get some professional help."

"What are you talking about? I don't need any help to treat the woman I love with care and compassion. Nobody has more control over me than I do. I am over this now! I will never harm you again."

"You need help. You need to see a psychiatrist or somebody like that. That's the only way you can get past this problem. Otherwise, you will always beat up anybody you love."

He didn't say anything for a while. I thought he had hung up.

"You really don't know me, do you?"

"I guess not."

"OK. I'll talk to you later." With that, Mark did hang up. I hoped that would be the last time he called.

I wandered into the den where my mother was watching TV.

"Mark cannot get off the same tune!" I complained, sitting on the sofa beside her.

"He'll come around." Mama put her arm around me as we sat and watched *The Carol Burnett Show* together.

Chapter 16

WHAT BECOMES OF THE BROKENHEARTED?

THE NEXT MORNING, I THOUGHT about the one interview I had set up. It was for the programming language that I had used in Atlanta. I actually preferred the programming language that I had used at my job in Columbus, but there were not a whole lot of companies seeking that skill.

I decided to call a friend from my old job to see if they had any openings that required my former skill. Such projects were still going on, but my friend didn't know if there were any openings. I decided to call the manager who was in charge of those projects.

Fortunately, the manager said they might have something. He promised to have HR call me and set up some meetings early the following week. Meanwhile, I followed up with the current leads I had.

"Smitty and Sheryl have been asking about you." Mark said when he called that night. He was speaking about his acquaintances that lived in his apartment complex.

"I hope you told them I had left you."

"No, I told them you were in Columbus visiting family."

"You should have told them the truth."

"I think Sheryl knows that something is wrong. I sense a mocking tone in her voice when she says 'Tell Maria I miss her' or when she asks, 'When is Maria coming back?'"

"If you tell her the truth, you won't have to worry about what she says."

"Hm." Mark let silence hang in the air for a bit. "Why did you marry me?"

"What?"

"Why did you marry me? What is the real reason?"

It was my turn to pause and think.

"I loved you. I thought we could build a good marriage, raise a nice family, and grow old together."

"You don't think that now?"

"No. All that is out of reach now."

"So you didn't marry me because you loved me. You married me for something else. What was it?"

"Nothing else."

Mark kept insisting that it was something else, that it couldn't have been love if it only lasted a few weeks. I finally became weary with his badgering me for the something else, and I bid him good night. But after I hung up, I started asking myself why I married him. Why didn't I just break up with him and move to Columbus instead of agreeing to marry him? I pondered whether or not something else was at work in my subconscious mind.

It wasn't okay to leave Atlanta because of boyfriend problems, but had I subconsciously thought that if he were my husband, it was okay to leave Atlanta? Or was it a higher calling than that?

I loved Mark enough to think that I could help him work through the challenges of his job, his insecurities about the woman he loved, and all the other things that weighed on him. I felt I was the quintessential black woman who could be a strong shoulder both for her man to lean on and to help him bear the burdens of life. That was required of us.

My mother and so many other women in my family had been that strong support for their husbands. I knew I could do it, too.

I really wanted to help him overcome this psychological problem that wasn't all his doing. His mother had let me in on the underlying factors of that problem sometime before our lunchtime fight. We had been sitting with his parents in the living room of their apartment one afternoon.

"Well, I've got to start working on these greens if we're going to have them later on," his mother said as she pushed against the sofa cushions and raised herself to a standing position.

"Is there something I can help you with?" I asked.

"Sure, come on in. We'll leave these menfolk to do whatever it is they do."

Her eyes sparkled as they usually did, while she stood at the sink full of water and collard greens. An excellent cook, she had worked for years in the kitchen of one of the public schools.

"I'm going to finish up this mess of greens, Maria. Why don't you put water in that pot and get the onions and the package of salt pork out of the fridge?"

Smiling, she went on, "How do y'all fix greens up in Ohio?"

"Well, actually, I had never fixed greens until I moved down here. Mark taught me how to make them."

"Oh, good. Then I don't have to explain anything to you if Mark taught you. He's always been a good cook." She smiled and the skin at the edges of her eyes crinkled, just like Mark's.

I found the salt pork in the refrigerator, opened the pack, and washed it in the second sink. Then I carefully cut the top layer crosswise in both directions as Mark had taught me.

"I really should have started on these greens before now. We'll use the pressure cooker to try to hurry this along. Everything else is ready to go—Oh! I forgot. Tell Mark to come in here."

I went back to the living room and called for Mark. Mark

and his father were talking about the television program they were watching.

"Your mom needs to see you."

"OK. Hold on, Daddy, and I'll be right back."

"Mark," she said as she looked up at him. "My goodness, I planned to make macaroni and cheese. I don't have any more macaroni, and I don't have enough cheese. Can you run to the store and get me a large box of macaroni and two blocks of cheddar cheese? And take your father with you. He needs to get out of that chair sometimes," she laughed.

"Sure, Mother."

As I heard Mark and his father heading out the front door, it occurred to me that this was the first time I had ever known them to go somewhere together.

"All he does is watch TV when he gets home," Mrs. Towns said. "It'll do him good to get out with his son every now and then."

She chatted as we worked on the greens, me peeling and cutting the onion, and Mrs. Towns taking the greens through their final wash.

"Why don't you get one of those big pots out and get the water ready for the macaroni? That way we can start the macaroni as soon as they get back."

I got the pot out; then I asked her a question.

"Mrs. Towns, do you know why Mark gets jealous and loses his temper about things he just imagines about me?"

She kept looking at the sink and washing greens for a while. I began to wonder if she heard me. Finally, she began speaking slowly in a lowered voice.

"My husband is a good man. He worked long hours as a janitor to bring in as much money as he could to provide for me and our five kids. But years ago, he used to beat me something terrible. Marky was always the child who was the angriest when that happened."

She paused, looking up at the ceiling. "He would put his arms around me to comfort me. And he would say 'Mother, I'm never going to do that to my wife!'"

Her words were caressing, like the tender memories of a much loved son.

"Then, later on, his brother got married." She looked serious suddenly while she stuffed some of the greens into the pressure cooker.

"That wife was a pistol! She cheated on him like a crazy woman!"

She picked up some more greens to wash.

"When Marky found out about it, he was real mad! 'Mother,' he would say, 'why doesn't Charles do something to stop her?' I had no answer for him."

"After that..." She gave a quick sigh that sounded like a huff. Her eyebrows hooded her eyes as she moved to get a towel. I felt a sudden sadness as I realized she had lost the sparkle in her eyes.

We heard someone at the front door yelling over the TV voices. "Hello? Hey?"

It was Mark's older brother. As he entered the kitchen, he smiled and said, "Where is everybody else? Did they get sucked into that TV screen Daddy's always glued to?"

The brightness returned to Mrs. Towns' eyes, and I didn't ever bring up that topic again. But that conversation helped me to realize that, as long as Mark was still in love with his old girlfriend, he never showed any jealousy toward me. It was only when he started telling me he loved me that the jealous accusations started. I wanted to help Mark make the connection, so he could finally enjoy a loving relationship without the stress of jealousy.

Chapter 17

ON MY OWN

Although I gave him no encouragement, Mark didn't miss a day calling me from Atlanta. Most days he called more than once.

He would always start the conversation with some pleasantries, asking me about my day and telling me about people we knew and things that were going on in Atlanta.

He always eventually worked his way to the same plea for me to return, and always I told him the same thing: he needed professional help. Every day he would get upset with me for suggesting that.

I wasn't sure why Mark wouldn't let himself see the real problem.

One day, before he hit me the second time, I was in his apartment alone listening to Donny Hathaway's album, *Extensions of a Man*, and making a meatloaf.

Among the songs on this album was the well-crafted instrumental *"I Love the Lord, He Heard My Cry."* The orchestra and choir in this particular song always took my mind to an imaginary meadow by a large lake. I easily envisioned myself enjoying the lushness of the greenery and the flow of animal and fish life around the water. In my mind, I was sitting down on a stump, looking around and thanking God for making scenes like this for mankind to enjoy.

Donny Hathaway's instrumental seamlessly merged into an up-tempo movement where I saw myself standing up and swirling around in a circle, arms outstretched, and full of happiness at where I was.

Then, just as suddenly, the cut changed into a slower tempo featuring Donny singing *"Someday We'll All Be Free."* In fact, Donny and I were singing as one that day, and I was smiling because his tenor voice was so rich and warm, and mine was—well, common, at best.

When Mark walked into the apartment, I smiled at him through the pass-through and kept on singing with Donny. Mark didn't seem happy, but I was exuberant as I swayed to the sexy saxophone interlude.

Instead of saying "hello," he said, "I heard you were in a car with a man. A man with a beard."

"Uh-uh. Not me," I assured him as I happily twirled into the hallway where he stood.

"It was a white car, a two-door Ford or a Chevy. He was a medium brown-skinned man!"

I stopped dancing. And I stopped smiling. "I haven't been in a car with any man but you since I met you. You know that."

I turned back into the kitchen with Mark following behind.

"Yes, you were. This person saw you!"

I turned around and stared at Mark. Now, only my analytical mind was spinning. *Why would someone tell him a lie like that? Who disliked him—or me—so much that they would make up some tall tale? Or, even if it had been true, who would just volunteer that* much *information to him?*

Then it hit me. *That much detail! Nobody told him that. Mark saw some bearded man in a car. Mark thought that might be somebody I would be interested in. So Mark decided to test the waters by accusing me of already being interested in that person.*

He had lit a cigarette and was standing in the only entry to the constricted kitchen.

"Mark," I said softly, "Nobody really told you that."

I paused before saying as tenderly as possible. "You just made that up yourself."

He blew out cigarette smoke from his mouth. I went on, speaking as calmly as I could. "Why would you do that?"

He thought for just a few seconds, taking another drag on his cigarette. Then he said, "I don't know."

He walked away and sat down in one of the chairs in the dining area.

Donny's song was over. I moved across the hall, into the room where the record player stood. The next album cut, *"Flying Easy,"* had started up. I just turned off the record player and went back to the kitchen to finish preparing the meal.

That was the only time that I had gotten Mark to address the fact that he was making up things.

But none of this was my concern anymore. I was about to interview with my former project leader and co-workers. I wanted to avoid embarrassing questions, so I decided to remove my customized wedding ring and to fill out any paperwork using my maiden name.

At the interview, I learned that they had a need for somebody who could program in both languages that I knew. It had not been formalized into a job opening yet, but they felt they could make this happen. For my part, it was the type of job I would really enjoy. A chance to do short-term programming projects for the emergency needs of the company. New challenges on a regular basis!

The other company that I interviewed with called back and made a formal offer. They gave me a couple of days to think it over.

Mark called that evening.

"Hello, Maria. How has your day gone?"

"Oh, it's gone very well. I got one job offer, and I'm pretty sure

I'm going to get another one from the place where I worked before I moved to Atlanta."

"And that's a good thing?"

"Yeah! Why not? My bills didn't disappear. And nobody lives rent-free. I need to contribute to this house since I'm living with my parents again."

"But you know that's not where you need to be. We have a marriage."

"Hey. We don't need to go over this again."

"Yes, we do. You said you love me. You couldn't love me if you're just going to walk away from me and give up on our marriage."

"Mark. You know why I walked away. I don't love you enough to lose my life because you're acting crazy! One of us has to have good sense."

"Crazy! That's what you want to say about me? That I'm crazy? That I don't have good sense?"

"No. When you imagine that I've been unfaithful and you act on that imagination by hitting me, that's acting crazy. You are the one who doesn't love me. You are the one who did this to our marriage. It all hangs on you!"

"Look, Maria. I love you. I'll do anything you ask. You are my queen, and I promise I will treat you like a queen forever. I'm at your command." He paused briefly before adding, "Queen Maria."

"Get some help."

"So I'm crazy."

"No. You just need some professional help. You cannot cure yourself of your imaginings on your own."

"You're right. I can only do this with you in my corner."

"I'm in your corner, but I'm in your corner in Columbus."

"We can't have a long-distance marriage."

"We don't have a marriage anymore!"

"So you really have given up on me. You never have loved me."

"I have loved you. I still love you. But it takes more than love."

"And you're not ready to give more than love."

"You're not ready."

"OK. I see where your head is. Take the easy way out. Try it for a week, if it doesn't work out, just give up. Throw that marriage away. Alright, Mrs. Towns. Thanks for letting me know just how important our marriage is to you."

"Mark, there is no guilt on my part. I was a good wife to you. A very good wife. You didn't do your part."

"If that's what you want to believe."

"That's a fact."

"OK. This conversation is going nowhere. I'll say goodbye for now."

"Alright, goodbye." In my mind I was thinking, *You can say goodbye forever!*

He hung up, and I was glad. I briefly considered not answering the phone anymore, but my mother and brother were still getting calls on this line. I had to keep answering until he figured out that I wasn't coming back.

But there was still that one problem. I had to go back at some point to get my car and my clothes. I hadn't figured out how to orchestrate that so there was as little drama as possible. Do I need to have somebody drive me down there, or should I go by plane since I'm bringing my car back? Should I tell him when I'm going to get my car and my clothes, or should I just show up and get my clothes? Then, if he's not home, who knows how long I'd have to wait for him to come back so that I could get my car. Do I need to take somebody with me? Whenever I tried to think it through, there never seemed to be a good solution.

Not only couldn't I figure out the logistics, but also I wasn't looking forward to the confrontation.

Earlier that day, I found out from relatives how to contact my cousin Kirk. I called him after talking to Mark.

"Kirk!" I said when he answered the phone. "This is Maria."

"Good to hear from you, Maria!"

"I've been wanting to talk to you—to explain what happened on the day of your parole."

"Yeah, I had wondered why you left me high and dry out there."

"Yeah, I'm so sorry. I had to leave Atlanta in a bit of a hurry that weekend. I left my husband."

"Wow, you did? That was a short marriage!"

"Yeah, unfortunately. My husband was insanely jealous, and he would act on that insanity."

"Act on it? Did he hit you?"

"Yes."

"Aw, Cuz. You don't have to put up with that from anybody. You were right not to stick around."

"I know."

"Well, I'm glad you're safely out of that. And don't feel bad about anything. It was more than okay not coming to get me for that reason. I waited about five or seven minutes that day. Then I figured you weren't coming, so I got on the next bus that came by the prison."

"That's good! I tried to call the prison long-distance and leave a message for you that I wouldn't be by. But they wouldn't take the message, even for someone going on parole the next day."

"Yeah, that place is a mess! But it's all behind me now. Life is good here, and I'm not going back there."

"Good for you, Cuz!"

We talked a while longer, then said our goodbyes.

I wondered if Kirk would be true to his word. I had heard that recidivism was high among former prisoners. We had become much closer during my stay in Atlanta than we had been during all those years when we lived in different cities. I cared deeply about his future now. We were both on the road to a brighter day. I really wanted him to stay on that road!

Chapter 18

"CAN YOU STAND THE RAIN?"

MARK'S LONG-DISTANCE CALL THE NEXT night started with his usual pleasantries.

"Did you have a good day?"

"I sure did."

"I did, too. I talked to Dr. Peters."

"Oh, yeah? How is he doing?" Dr. Peters was a physician–lawyer–psychiatrist–author whose physical appearance always reminded me of Louis Farrakhan. Mark had introduced me to him during a party. We had run into Dr. Peters again at a couple of workshops. He was well-respected in Atlanta and, as a result we sometimes caught him being interviewed on TV or radio shows.

"He's doing well. I talked to him about our situation."

"You did?" I was shocked because Mark didn't really want any of his friends to know that he was an abuser. "How much of our situation did you talk to him about?"

"All of it. I didn't leave anything out."

"Did you tell him that you were basing your actions on things that you just imagined? Things that never happened?"

"I did."

"And what did he say?"

"Well, he said he was surprised to know that about me. But he did say that, as a psychiatrist, he would be willing to help us."

"You mean he would be willing to help you."

"Me. Us. We're a team."

"We *were* a team."

"We can be a team again. Maria, I'll only do this for you, for our marriage. If you're not coming back, there's no point in me doing this."

"You need to do this for yourself. You cannot have a meaningful relationship—ever—if you don't do this for yourself."

"I don't want any other relationship. I want ours. If I cannot be in a relationship with you, then I don't want to be in any relationship."

"Mark, that is short-sighted. Do this for yourself. Get well so you can have a life, a marriage, a family."

"I want to get well so I can have all that with you. You wanted me to get help. I will do this because you want it."

"But you should want it, too! Don't you want to be happy?"

"I am happy when I'm with you."

"Hah! You never acted like it. All you wanted to do was believe that I was cheating on you."

"I don't want to act like that. I know you never cheated on me, and you are the one I want to live happily with for the rest of my life."

I sighed deeply. Here was the man I loved, ready to do sessions with a psychiatrist. Not for himself, because he dreaded thinking he was not right in the head. But for me. Because I had told him that's what he needed to do.

Mark went on. "If you love me, if we ever had anything good between us, come back and let's rebuild our marriage together. Help me get through these sessions. This therapy is not going to be easy. Work with me so I can be the man you deserve."

"You're asking a lot. You're asking me to trust you again. I don't think I can do that."

"I'm trustworthy because I don't want us to break up. I don't want to lose you. I don't think you want to lose me either. We can show the world that a brother and sister in love can work together to save a good marriage."

When I hung up the phone that night, I knew that I would be talking to Dr. Peters.

Chapter 19

THINK

THE NEXT DAY I RECEIVED a verbal offer from my former employer who said an official written offer would follow. Delighted, I told them I would get back with them.

Meanwhile, I called Information in Atlanta, looking for Dr. Peters' office number. Then I dialed his number and told his receptionist that I was calling long-distance to speak to Dr. Peters. She put me through to him.

"Dr. Peters, this is Maria, Mark Towns' wife."

"Yes, Maria. How are you doing?"

"I'm doing fine," I said. "How are you?"

"Oh, I am doing well."

"I'm calling you because Mark said he talked to you about his jealousy and the way that he responds to it."

"Yes, we did talk about that."

"He said he told you everything.....Did he tell you that he once hit me so hard that the bruise on my face didn't go away for a week?"

"Yes."

"Did he tell you that he tried to strangle me and that's when I finally left?"

"Yes." He sighed. "I must tell you that all of this was so shocking to me. I always felt that Mark was a stellar young man. I had no idea he was hiding this kind of secret inside."

"I'm sure that none of Mark's friends is aware of this problem. Can you tell me what you recommended to him?"

"Well, I told him that I could work with him, if he wanted me to, but the results would all depend on him. He must come in every week for the sessions, first off."

"If he does, can he be cured?"

"People can be cured of this issue, but it is not a quick fix. It takes a long time, and the person must want to be healed."

"How long is 'long?'"

"That's not something I can estimate. Each case is different. The hardest part is to get the client to stick with it and to actively seek to do better."

"I see."

"Maria, I want you to know in no uncertain terms that there are *no guarantees* here. A cure is possible, but it's all on Mark."

"He says he is willing to do it."

"Yes, he is saying that because he really wants you to come back."

"I know."

"Know this, too: all men will say whatever they think is necessary to get their woman back. I'm not telling you to come back or to stay away. That decision is totally up to you. But I am telling you that the success of the treatment depends totally on Mark. It does not depend on you!"

"I care about him getting better. I still love him. "

"I understand that. But you have to understand that he is grasping at straws to get you back. How long have you been gone?"

"I left a week ago as of this past Saturday."

"That's not long at all. If you were to come right back, he would have no reason to start and follow through on therapy. He will have gotten what he wants, and he can just keep on doing what he did before."

"So what are you saying?"

"If you decide to go back to him, you must make him wait. You must make him feel the painful effects of what he has done."

"Like another three weeks?"

"I doubt that's long enough either. I cannot and will not tell you if or when to go back. I'm just telling you that you cannot give him immediate gratification. This is a very serious offense. He *must* endure the awful consequences of his terrible actions. That is a part of the treatment, too."

"I understand, Dr. Peters. Look, I don't want to hold you up any longer. Thank you so much for talking to me."

"You're welcome, Maria, and good luck. You deserve to be treated like a lady. No woman deserves abuse."

I hung up the phone thinking about Mark's situation. Even his friend, Dr. Peters, didn't empathize with him on this one. Mark was not only broken up, but also all alone. Everyone, including his wife, had deserted him.

The reality was that, even though I hated how Mark had treated me because of his jealous imaginings, I missed being held and loved by Mark.

The first time we made love, his tenderness had caught me off guard. Nothing was rushed. He slowly traced a sizzling trail of fire up my leg and around my pelvis with the tips of his finger. At the same time, his tongue titillated the inner surfaces of my lips. My heart rate and hunger far exceeded his by the time we actually made love. Maybe because he was in his 30s, he had learned the importance of slow foreplay in ensuring the satisfaction of a woman.

And that wasn't the only surprise. Mark knew a variety of ways to make love, all of which seemed designed for my maximum pleasure. I doubted that many other men knew the lovemaking secrets that Mark held. Sometimes I wondered if he knew how special he was in that area. If he had known, he would never have been so suspicious of losing the women that he loved.

The ringing phone interrupted my thoughts, which had wandered into territories best left alone at that time. I figured it was Mark calling.

"Hello?"

"Hello, Mrs. Towns."

"Hi, Mark," I said rather indifferently.

"What was your day like?"

"It was pretty good."

"Yeah?"

"Yeah. My old employer made me an offer today. It is a really challenging position that I know I will love."

"Love more than me?"

"Two different things."

"Not really. Every father, every mother has to figure out if their jobs are more important than their families."

"Well, I'm not a mother."

"You're a wife, my wife. That's the first step to being a mother. But maybe that's not anything you really wanted. Maybe being a wife is not anything that you wanted."

"And maybe being a husband isn't anything you wanted."

"You don't know how much I want that. For you and me."

"Yeah," I said curtly. Then I went on. "Look, Mark, I spoke to Dr. Peters today."

"You did?" He sounded honestly surprised.

"Yes."

"Why?"

"I wanted to see if you had told him the whole story. And, I wanted to know what his thoughts were on healing."

"And so, what did you think after talking to him?"

"He said it's all on you. You have to want to get better. You have to attend all the sessions. You have to see it through until the end."

"Yes, and I'm going to do that!"

"Can you do that? This is his job. He doesn't do it for free."

"It doesn't matter. Our marriage is worth saving."

"I didn't say it would save our marriage. I didn't say that I would come back."

There was a short pause before Mark went on.

"Maria, you are the only person I would do this for. I don't want any other woman. I want you, my wife. You are worth the effort—no matter what the cost is."

"I don't know that you are really thinking about the cost. It is time and money. I don't know, you may get upset and think it's not doing any good, and then you will stop, and you wouldn't be healed."

"No—no. When I see what I almost lost, when I see how I almost destroyed our marriage. That is the reminder that will keep me going. I can't risk losing you again."

"You're acting like I've decided to come back."

"No, I'm not. I'm just praying to God that you will come back. I have been praying for another chance. I want this marriage to be whole again. I don't want to mess it up."

When we ended the conversation, I continued to emphasize to Mark that I had not agreed to come back. All I was interested in was that he see Dr. Peters and go through the treatment. I was not agreeing to be there with him while he went through it.

"How did it go with Mark?" It was my mother popping her head into my room.

I was lying on the bed on my back, one arm draped across my forehead.

"I am thinking about going back, but I didn't let him know that."

Chapter 20

GET IT TOGETHER

"What made you consider that option?" Mama asked. I sighed. "I don't know. I still love Mark. I hate what he did to me, but when he's not accusing me of being with other men, he is very sweet to me and we have a great relationship."

"Um-hm." My mother moved to sit down on the edge of my bed. I sat up in the bed and drew my knees up to my chin so I could give her more sitting room.

"Mark said he would go through therapy sessions with a psychiatrist that we know," I said.

"Do you trust that person? Do you trust Mark?"

"I talked to the psychiatrist, and he said it is possible for a person to be healed from being abusive, but the weight of the healing is on the person and it's a long process."

"What about trusting Mark?"

"Mark is all torn up about this breakup. He says he will do the psychiatry sessions."

"Don't forget that men say *anything* when they really want to get back with you." My mother sounded like an echo chamber to Dr. Peters.

"I know," I struggled inwardly to say my real thoughts. "I don't want to be single and hit the party scene again. I am ready to be settled, to raise a family."

I looked up at the ceiling and wrapped my arms around my knees. "If it is possible for Mark to be healed, I'd prefer to be married to him." I didn't know how else to explain my change of heart.

"I just don't know," I finally said.

"What is it that you 'don't know?'"

"I don't know if he'll do the therapy. He doesn't really think anything is wrong with him. Or should I say, he doesn't see this as a sickness. He sees it as something he can control now that he knows the effect it has on me...what if he thinks he's got it under control, and he stops going to the psychiatrist? And what if he starts beating me up again? There is no way I want that kind of marriage….even with Mark."

"What do you think you'll do about your dream job offer? Are you thinking about passing that up?"

"That's the other thing. It's the kind of challenge I've always wanted! They know me here. They know I can do it. I'd have to fight my way up for years to get that kind of job in Atlanta—once I got a job in Atlanta."

"You said they told you that they'd be glad to have you back at your job in Atlanta."

"Yeah, but I think I'd be too embarrassed to go back there, especially since I would still be with Mark." I sighed. "I don't know!"

"Well, pray on it; sleep on it."

When I said my nightly prayers, I did include a short request concerning Mark. "Lord, you know the situation, and I am thoroughly confused. You know how Mark has treated me. I wanted our marriage to work. I believed that I was a good wife who honored our marriage vows. I've done all I know how to do. He did not do right by me. Now he is finally willing to get help. He's all alone, and nobody is in his corner. Help me to do the right thing by Mark."

The next morning I padded into the kitchen in a robe and slippers. The smell of coffee brewing always reminded me of my parents sitting in the kitchen in the morning, and this morning I inhaled the familiar smell. This time, only my mother was in the kitchen, preparing her breakfast before leaving for work.

After greeting her, I sat down at the kitchen table and crossed my legs.

"Mama," I said slowly. "I'm going back to Atlanta. Going back to Mark."

She looked over at me briefly, then lowered her gaze to the skillet where she was scrambling eggs.

I had gotten the hard part out of my mouth. Now I went on more confidently. "If he's willing to do the therapy, then I'm willing to go back and make this marriage work."

"What makes you so sure?"

"I'm not sure that I'm sure," I chuckled nervously. "I just need to do the right thing. And I think the right thing is to give our marriage my all if Mark's going to give it his all."

She carefully lifted the eggs out of the skillet onto the plate.

"So what is your plan?"

"Well … the psychiatrist said, if I go back, to make him wait before I do. I've already been gone 10 days, so I figure I can go back in four weeks and that will be a long enough separation."

"And what will you do during the wait?"

"Um. I'll probably get a temporary job so I can earn some money. I'll need money for a ticket back to Atlanta."

"So you're going to let your dream job go?"

"Yes, unfortunately. I'll have to let them know of my decision in a couple of days."

"And what will you do if Mark starts being abusive again?" She took a sip of her coffee and removed her toast from the toaster while I considered the question again.

"If he is abusive again, if the therapy doesn't work, I'll have to give up on the marriage and leave him. For good." I frowned as I considered him falling back into that behavior. "But I think he's for real this time. He's really broken up about the fact that he hurt me."

Mama said her grace and began eating. "Do you think they like you enough to hold the job here while you find out if it's going to work with Mark?"

"That would certainly be ideal, but I didn't tell them I had gotten married. I signed everything under my maiden name."

"Oh."

"I'd be afraid to ask. If they really want to hire somebody else, I'd be holding them up for a few weeks."

"Well," she said as she took another bite of eggs, "Why don't you ask if you can have a delayed start? Give yourself enough time to see if Mark's going to revert to his old ways or not."

"What do you mean?"

"Well, you want to go back when?"

"In four weeks."

She talked between bites of food.

"Do you think two more weeks down there would be enough time for you to know if he's going to be better?"

"I believe so."

"Then ask them if they'd be willing for you to start in six weeks."

"Do you think they would let me do that?"

"You can ask."

"Why would they agree to that?"

"Well, if it's really *you* that they want, and if they weren't actively trying to hire somebody before you came along, they should be willing."

"I don't know what reason I'd give them for waiting so long."

"Well, you don't have to make up anything. You *do* need to go back and pack up your belongings and get your car. As far as they know, you might have other loose ends to tie up in Atlanta, like terminating your apartment lease and things of that nature."

"You are brilliant, Mama!"

"No, not really. But I have to get out of here and get to my job. We can talk more later."

I accepted the job offer on the condition that I could have six weeks to go back to Atlanta and complete my transition to Columbus. They were more than happy to give me the extra time.

Mark called the next night, sounding as positive as usual.

"Well, Mrs. Towns, how was your day?"

"Oh, it was fine."

"And your grandmother?"

"She's doing the same."

"Well, I pray for her. I'm hoping she won't be in any pain."

"I'd like that, too. But she continues to be in pain for periods of time."

"I know, and I'm sorry about that."

"Me, too."

"You know, I told you last night that I was praying for our marriage to be whole again?"

"Yes, I remember."

"I want that more than anything!"

"If you really do want that more than anything, then your prayers have been answered. I am coming back so we can both give it another try."

"Are you really, Maria?" He was incredulous.

"Yes."

"That is fantastic!" I could hear the excitement in Mark's voice. "I won't let you down this time, I promise!"

I chuckled because I was just as pleased, too.

"When? When will you be back?" he asked.

I got serious then. "Mark, I'm not coming back right now.

What you did was terrible, and you can't just get me back with the flick of your wrist."

"I understand that, Maria. I miss you terribly."

"Yeah, I miss you, too. But we'll have to miss each other for a while."

He was serious now. "What is 'a while?'"

"I'll be back in a month."

"That's a long time. You've already been gone so long."

"I haven't been gone that long. And I'm probably coming back too soon for you to really feel the bad effects of your actions."

It was his turn to chuckle. "Trust me. I feel the effects of those actions enough to never do them again."

"Then you can wait."

"I don't want to, but I can. It's far better than the possibility of us never getting back together again. A month it is! "

"But, Mark, this all hinges on you going to the therapy sessions with Dr. Peters. If you're not going to keep doing that, I'm not going to come back."

"Maria, I want to do those sessions. I *will* do those sessions dutifully," he promised.

"OK, that's the deal." I earnestly believed that he not only could change, but also *wanted* to change.

"You know what? I'll do that and more. You'll get the husband that you deserve this time!"

Chapter 21

SHARE MY WORLD

Now I began looking forward to Mark's nightly call. I didn't press him to start the therapy sessions yet, because I knew that he had racked up a huge phone bill with all the long-distance calls he had made to me. My plan was for us to pay that big bill down and then get started on the extra, but necessary, expense of meeting with Dr. Peters.

Mark had finally caught up on all his overdue bills before I left, so I felt we could eke out enough from his pay for the sessions. Meanwhile, I would look for another job and, once I found one, we would be in a somewhat comfortable position. Definitely not rich, but comfortably paying our living expenses.

I called about an ad in the newspaper for temporary workers in computer programming. However, when I interviewed with the temporary service, I learned that they didn't really have any temporary programming jobs at the moment. They noted that I had worked summer jobs as a typist when I was in college and asked if I would be interested in a clerk-typist job on a temporary basis.

It wasn't long before I started a three-week temporary job in the Ohio EPA as a receptionist-typist. This would allow me to generate some money to buy a plane ticket back to Atlanta, keep paying on my bills, and have a little extra change when I got back to Atlanta.

Every night, Mark would call me to talk about the happenings in Atlanta and with folks we knew. I told him that he didn't need to call every night but, deep inside, I was glad that he did. I missed him terribly, and it was clear that he was missing me. We could worry about the phone bill later.

Most times, I didn't have any important news to share with Mark because he didn't know the people I interacted with but, during my last week in Columbus, I did have something.

"We had a little bit of excitement at work today," I said.

"Really? What happened?"

"Well, we have a short hallway that separates the reception area from the typing pool at the back of our section. The EPA reps all have offices along that hallway."

"Yeah?"

"Well, today all the reps were in a meeting. I left my area so that I could deliver some typing to the typists at the end of the hall. I stayed back there a few minutes just talking, and then I headed back to the front."

"OK."

"Well, there was a man—a young black man—walking back down the hall in the same direction I was going in. He had never come all the way to the end of the hall, and there was nobody for him to stop and see in the hall—because they were all gone."

"Um-hm."

"He seemed shocked to hear footsteps behind him, and he turned his head real fast to see who it was."

"Did he say anything to you?"

"No, he didn't. I wondered if he had gone into any of the offices and stolen anything, but I really didn't want to think that. I mean,

I didn't know the man, and he could have been a maintenance worker or a mail clerk or anything."

"So what did you find out?"

"Well, after the reps came back, one of them came out of her office and said her billfold was gone. She asked me had I seen anybody suspicious around."

"Did you tell her about that guy?"

"Yeah. I felt bad that he had been a bad guy, and that I didn't want to think that about him, so I didn't try to stop him."

"Well, you can't just assume somebody is bad."

"I know. When I was telling the story, one of the reps asked me if I said something like 'Can I help you?' I had to admit that I said nothing."

"Well, what did they do?"

"They said that they'd been bothered before with somebody coming in the building and stealing from random offices on various floors. They felt it was probably this same person again, but nobody had ever seen him before."

"So now you're the only eyewitness."

"Yeah, and you know how I really can't remember faces."

"Right. You're so bad at that!"

"The police brought in a mug book and asked me if any of the guys was the one I saw."

"Did you find him?"

"You know that was the worst experience. There were a couple of guys who could have been him, based on their skin complexion and haircuts, but I didn't feel that I could positively identify one of them. I mean, can you imagine being hauled into jail just because you looked 'something like' the guy who stole something?"

I thought about my cousin Kirk. I said, "Once you get caught for something and your picture gets in the mug book, you're always liable to be pulled into a lineup just because it could have been you. How unfair is that?"

"Yeah, that's the way the system works. Once convicted, always a suspect."

"Well, I ended up saying that I couldn't be sure that it was any one of those men in the mug book. But you know what the underlying thought probably was?"

"Oh, I'm well aware of that thought. They don't know you, so you could have been the one who stole the billfold."

"Right! If I was white, it would never have crossed anyone's mind. But I'm black. I'm only there until the end of this week. I am a suspect, even though nobody said it."

"Yeah, well, nobody *said* it, so you just keep doing your job and get on back down here. It'll be all right."

Chapter 22

WHAT YOU WON'T DO FOR LOVE

A COUPLE OF DAYS LATER, I was actually boarding the plane back to Atlanta. I had typed a letter regarding my new job offer, saying that I had returned to Atlanta and gotten married and that, as excited as I was about the job, I would have to refuse it.

I had stamped and sealed the letter. It was dated for two weeks after my return, and I would only mail it if Mark seemed to be headed on the right path during those two weeks.

As the plane landed on that Friday night, I was as giddy as a teenager about to go on a date with someone she had a crush on. I actually had the fluttering feeling of butterflies in my stomach.

When I got off the plane and saw Mark standing at the gate, dressed in his typical sports jacket and tie apparel, I felt my heart jump in my chest. Mark smiled broadly and kissed me on the lips.

"How was the flight?"

"It was fine!" I replied.

We put one arm around each other, delight dancing in our eyes, as we talked and walked through the airport terminal on our way to get my small bag from the baggage claim.

When I got to the apartment, I couldn't wait to open the front closet and greet Leta and Hasana again. I leaned down and gave both of them big hugs, happy to feel their curly fur against my cheeks. Mark stood aside with his hand on one hip.

"They missed you, but not half as much as I did!"

I played with the dogs a bit more as Mark took my bag to the bedroom. He called over his shoulder, "Are you hungry?"

"No, we had a meal on the plane. I'm fine."

He came back down the hall. "You want to go out tonight?"

"No. I just want to be here with you."

He smiled, and we kissed again. "I was hoping you would say that."

We made love repeatedly that night. It was beautiful and exciting, just as I had remembered it.

The next morning, we were lounging around the house, eating a leisurely breakfast. It was almost like a honeymoon. Mark didn't want to go anywhere else, and neither did I. We were happy just being together. No accusations. No more apologies. Just starting on a promise of a better life. That evening, Mark had a social commitment that the both of us attended.

It was Sunday before I finally approached Mark on the subject of how we could finance the sessions with Dr. Peters. Mark had not started the sessions yet, and we needed to get those started quickly if we were going to make this marriage work.

We were sitting at the kitchen table when I said, "I know that we must have a huge phone bill with all the times you called me."

Mark's eyes widened, but there was a smile lingering behind them. "You don't know how huge!"

"Yeah. Well, I know we need to start paying that down first."

He nodded.

"I need to start looking for a job. I wanted to talk to you about something I encountered while I was in Columbus. Some places have temporary jobs for computer programmers. I think I would really like the challenge of having different jobs, different challenges on a regular basis. What do you think?"

"If that's what you want, then do it."

"Of course, we'll have to live on your salary until I find the connection in Atlanta for a job like that."

"Yeah. Well, there's something you need to know, Maria."

"OK."

"I lost my job at the Housing Authority."

His words thundered down on my head like the falling timber and bricks of a building being bombed.

"What?" I exclaimed. "When did that happen?"

"Two weeks ago. It was another blow that I wasn't ready for. I was devastated over not being with you, and I really couldn't handle losing the job, too."

"Was it because of the friction between you and the lady in your office?"

"No!"

"Then what happened?"

"They lost the funding for the program that I came in on. All of the new folks were let go."

"Why didn't you tell me?"

"You know why. I was afraid you wouldn't come back if you knew that."

In my mind, I seriously wondered if I would have come back. We couldn't make it if neither of us was working. But then I remembered how I had started feeling sorry for all the things that were going against Mark. This would have just been another thing to make me have sympathy for Mark. Yes, I would have come back anyway, but I would have preferred knowing the whole truth. Regardless, I was here now and I needed to be strong and support him.

"I don't love you for your job," I said soothingly. "The job was never the issue. The abuse was."

"I know that now, but you know that I don't want to lose you. I came *so close* to losing you. I couldn't risk it again."

I rested my elbow on the table and leaned my head on my hand. "OK. So now neither one of us has a job. When's your last pay coming in?"

"I picked it up a week ago Friday."

My heart beat rapidly because I knew, without asking, that Mark had spent most of that money already. *Just keep thinking rationally,* I told myself.

"Are you looking for something else?" I asked him.

"You know I am. I've got feelers out among all my friends."

"OK. So I need to rethink my job plans because we're going to need some money quicker than I thought."

Mark got up from his seat and came beside mine. He knelt down and put his arms around me. "I love you."

"I love you, too." I sighed as I rubbed one hand over his neatly shaved Afro. "And we both need jobs."

The long-distance calls over the past six weeks had skyrocketed our phone bill to over $200. Not only that but, as the mail came in, it became clear that Mark had not paid the rent or other utility bills in my absence.

I was concerned about the appointments with Dr. Peters since we couldn't afford them right now. But the real pressing issue was paying the ongoing bills and rent.

"Mark, why didn't you pay these bills?" I asked him.

"I don't know, Maria. My mind was only on one thing and that was you. I've been in bad shape about bills before, but I don't know when I've ever been so low in spirit. I'm sorry."

"Well, I'm going to need to go to a temporary agency here and see if I can get a quick typing job. At least I'll get paid the first week I work."

"And I'm hunting for work, too. We'll get back on our feet."

Mark drove me to the temp agency the next day and, fortunately, they had plenty of jobs available. I told them that I needed a three-week assignment. Within one day, I got a secretarial job working with the Atlanta NAACP office.

The secretarial job generated some quick cash so that I could try to catch up on some bills.

Meanwhile, since Mark had not made any jealous accusations, I mailed off the letter saying that I would not be accepting the dream job after all. Things weren't perfect in our marriage, but at least the jealousy was gone.

Chapter 23

UNBREAKABLE

About a week after my return, Mark left the apartment, and I was there with the dogs in the bedroom. I had washed my two garter belts, knowing that I had an old garter belt in my junky lingerie drawer in case the other two didn't dry out by the next morning. As I dug through the silky belongings, my fingers touched a small slip of paper with some writing on it. It was not my handwriting, and I stopped to see why it was there.

The note on the paper read:

> Hey, Sister. Your man has been playing you and sleeping with somebody else—me! Call me and I'll fill you in.

A first name and a phone number were written at the bottom of the note. I stumbled backward onto the bed, completely bewildered. Who was this person, and how did this note get in my bedroom drawer?

My breathing became short and quick as I stared at the note and re-read it several times. Finally, I reasoned that the note could not have been there before I left Mark since there were so few times when he was in the house and I was not.

Obviously, Mark had brought someone in the apartment while I was in Columbus! Even though he was calling me regularly, he still had time to go out and find somebody to satisfy his sexual needs.

This, I thought, *is what happens when you walk away from your marriage. Especially when the other person believes that you are not coming back!*

Try to think through this, Maria, I told myself. I worked hard at taking a couple of deep breaths since my heart was racing. *First thing: I am not going to call this woman and give her the pleasure of gloating over how she had my man in bed!*

Second thing—the phone rang and jarred my thoughts. I slowly picked it up and said, "Hello."

It was Mark. "Hi, what cha doing?"

"I—I—I—"

I was still on the verge of hyperventilating.

"What's wrong?" he asked.

"I….reading a note …. from some woman."

"What note? What woman?"

"Some woman who says… she was in bed with you."

"What?"

"The note was in my lingerie drawer."

"What?" he said again. "What does the note say exactly?"

I read the note to him.

"I'll be right there."

I stared at the note again as I hung up the phone. I couldn't imagine that anyone would really be mean-spirited enough to leave that type of message. Was she hoping to break us up? Well, yeah, evidently that was her purpose.

My eyes were hopelessly fixed on the note, with a million thoughts running through my brain. I began to wonder if Jean was back. Jean had been attracted to Mark while he and I were dating, and before the abuse started. Most of Mark's female friends respected our relationship and didn't flirt with Mark. But Jean had been so bold as to show up at his apartment with her overnight bag, planning to spend the night with him. Mark claimed not to know that she was planning that. I refused to leave his apartment as long as she was there, and he ended up having a serious talk with her about our relationship. I never saw Jean again after that event.

I re-read the note, slowly, and decided that it wasn't from Jean. She would have taken great joy in leaving her real name and letting me know that she got to my man.

But, if not Jean, who and why?

The dogs rushed to the front door. Mark had made it back within 10 minutes.

He bounded to the bedroom where I still sat, his mouth fixed in a short, straight line. His eyes were serious as he saw that I was still holding onto the note.

"Let me see that."

I handed it to him. He read it quickly, tucked it in his pocket, and said, "I'll be back."

I knew that he was going to see that person, whoever she was. I really didn't care. I was back. She was out. Whatever indiscretion Mark had while I was gone could be forgiven since I knew who he really wanted—the person he had begged every day to come back.

I dusted the bedroom furniture and mopped the kitchen floor. None of those things needed work, but I was numbly going through the motions, any motions, just to stop dealing with those questions in my head.

Mark came back home within the hour. He said nothing about the note or the woman. I said nothing either. I felt certain that whoever she was, she would never be back in our lives again.

And I forced all my questions out of my head now that I realized Mark was not going to address them.

Chapter 24

SPOTLIGHT

AT THE END OF THE three weeks at the NAACP, I was eager to see if I could get some better-paying work as a programmer. The problem was that the phone company wanted more money than I had available to pay. It wasn't long before they cut off our phone service.

"Mark, I need to have a number where these companies can reach me if they are interested in hiring me as a temporary programmer."

"Yeah, I know."

"The only thing I can think of is to start using an answering service and to put its number on my resume."

"How would you know if they had calls for you?"

"I am not sure. I think they should be willing to hold my messages until I call in every day to check with them. I could use the pay phone across the street."

"That sounds good. I could use the same service for the job applications that I fill out."

"Yeah, let me check the yellow pages and see how much these services cost."

I talked to a couple of services via the pay phone and found that they were reasonably priced. They would answer the phone by saying their phone number. When the caller stated who they were looking for, the answering service would simply say that the person was out of the office and ask the caller to leave a message.

So I signed up for an answering service. I sent out resumes and dutifully checked with the service every day to see if I was getting any response. Day after day, there were no messages—not for Mark, not for me.

I had written my parents and told them that the phones had been turned off. I truthfully explained that it was because of the huge long-distance bills that Mark had run up and because his employer had let him go. I gave them the answering service number to call when they wanted to get in touch with me.

Very quickly, I received a phone message from them. I had to wait until that evening when I knew they would both be home to call. I couldn't afford to pay for the long-distance call from the phone booth, so I made a collect call to the main house line. I prayed that the line would be open, and it was.

The operator announced my call to my parents, "You have a collect call from Maria Towns. Will you accept the charges?"

"Yes," I heard my father say, just before he called for my mother and brother to pick up the extensions so that they could join the call.

"So what exactly happened? Why did Mark lose his job?" My father was anxious, asking the question almost before the others could pick up.

I briefly explained the circumstances.

He immediately said, "I need to help Mark get that training school started down there!"

I had forgotten all about the training school conversation they had had. Some years ago, Dad and a fellow pastor had started the Columbus Area Development and Training School, known as CADATS. This was right after the major civil rights thrusts of the mid-60s, so Corporate America was very interested in how to increase minority hiring.

The two ministers met with local businesses in order to get donations of office and mechanical equipment. They also received donations of money, instructors, and an old building that was soon renovated and ready for classes. The training school had successfully trained scores of folks whom the corporations were then anxious to hire.

My father always enjoyed a good debate and, during our 1972 Thanksgiving visit, he was impressed by Mark's impassioned conversations about the country's social ills. Dad had never really liked any of the dates who came to my house, but I saw that he was impressed with Mark. All of my dates had been well-mannered men who could carry on polite conversation. But, because my father just grunted while peering at them through his glasses, most of them never tried to engage him in any type of discussion.

Before Mark and I ended our Thanksgiving visit, my father told Mark about CADATS. He wanted to open the same type of school in Atlanta and asked Mark if he knew anyone he could talk to. Of course, Mark knew lots of people, and he encouraged my father to come and promote the idea in Atlanta.

"I can only start the talks and get the initial setup going," Dad said. "I need someone to do the day-to-day operation and fundraising. You see, my health—," my father scoffed before continuing.

"My health won't allow me to stay there and do it for weeks or months at a time." Dad had emphysema from decades of smoking. We could hear his labored breathing whenever he walked through the house. As a result, he couldn't walk or be active for long periods of time. He was driving less and utilizing my brother as his driver whenever possible.

"Don't worry," Mark said. "I can do all the legwork for you while you're back in Columbus."

"Good! That's what I needed to know. I'll be talking more with you so we can put this together."

Now, almost a year later, my father was even more interested because this school could provide Mark with a needed salary, if he would be the chief fundraiser and the chief executive officer.

I wanted a more immediate income for Mark, especially since I remembered that corporate talks took place during the daytime hours. Mark couldn't work a job *and* solicit the school funding. But my father was enthusiastic about the idea of an Atlanta version of the school. I knew that, in spite of his health challenges, he would soon be in Atlanta, talking to corporate heads.

About a week after talking to my parents, I got a call in response to one of the resumes that I had sent out. I returned the call to a Mr. Barker. He wanted me to come in for an interview, so we agreed on a date and time. I was excited at this development and ran back to the apartment to tell Mark.

He had not secured any employment. All the money that I had made at the NAACP had been used to put a tiny dent in the bills and to buy food. We really needed this prospect.

On the day of the interview, I got out of the car and told Mark that he could meet me back at the same drop-off spot in two hours. The interview location was downtown, but it was on the opposite end of downtown from where I had worked before. Hopefully, I would not see any of my former co-workers and have to offer an explanation about my marriage.

"OK." Mark responded. "I've got to run an errand. I'll try to get a spot in this general area when I come back."

"No problem," I said. It was a crisp, cool morning, without a single cloud in the sky. I noticed a couple of benches in the area where I could wait for Mark if he had not returned by the time my interview ended.

I walked into the reception area of the building and asked for Mr. Barker.

While I sat and waited, I hoped that he wouldn't suddenly

become disinterested in my skills when he saw me. That had happened when I first interviewed at Southern Railway. The HR representative almost dropped the cigar from his mouth when he saw me. I didn't know then that they didn't have any black female programmers. He had talked to me for a short while, then told me that they didn't have any openings.

Fortunately, an employment agency had sent me to Southern Railway. When I reported what had happened, they immediately called HR, and I was returned for another interview with the person HR should have sent me to.

Even with that experience, I felt confident in this interview. I had dressed in a navy blue tweed suit with a white knit top underneath. The suit had a flared mini-skirt that was an appropriate length for the styles of the day; plus, I wore navy blue tights just to be on the safe side.

When I applied at Southern Railway, I had a large, curly, Angela-Davis-style Afro which I thought looked cute and sexy. Mark had gone with me to the barber shop one day when I went for a trim and, unbeknownst to me, had instructed the barber to give me a close-cut Afro.

I still wore my hair closely cut, even though it was a year later. I was hoping that this cut helped me to look like a serious businesswoman, someone who could turn around one or more short-term programming assignments for Mr. Barker.

Mr. Barker gave me a warm welcome and reviewed my resume with me. He asked me a few interview questions and told me about the kind of work that his department did.

As he concluded the interview, he said, "You know, Maria, you have a good work history and the kind of skills we need."

I eagerly nodded.

"Unfortunately we don't have a need for a temporary programmer." My heart sank.

He kept talking. "But we do have a need for a full-time

programmer. Would you be interested in coming on board for something like that? We have a variety of new projects that could use your expertise."

I was desperate at this point. Past due bills loaded up our mailbox, and we were behind on the rent. I needed work, and I needed it quick.

"Yes, Mr. Barker. That would work fine for me. I like new challenges, and the kind of projects you've described would be very interesting to me."

"Good. Then I'll get the paperwork to HR, and we will send you a formal written offer. When would you be available to start?"

"Well, I don't have any pending assignments, so I could start whenever you want me."

"OK. They'll work out a suitable start date and let you know what it will be when they send out the written offer." He got up from his seat, shook my hand, and started leading me to the front door of the building.

As we walked, he told me little tidbits about the facility such as the working hours, cafeteria, and break times. Once we got to the door of the building, he walked me out to the front steps. I said goodbye, shook his hand, and started down the steps.

"Oh!" he said suddenly. "I wanted to tell you that the employees generally park over there." He pointed to a parking lot that was right across the street from the building.

"The fees are pretty good, and they have a monthly contract that gives you a break on the daily fees. As long as you are paying the daily or monthly rate, they don't mind if you take the car out for lunch or whatever."

"Okay. Thank you for the tip. I'll look forward to hearing from you!"

I walked down the remaining steps and scanned the area with my eyes. I saw that Mark had the car parked in the nearby general location he had indicated. I headed to the car and was all smiles.

"I've got the job!" I happily told Mark.

"You think so?" Mark was not smiling.

"Yeah. It's for permanent work. They will send me a formal letter in the mail."

"Who was that guy that you were talking to?"

"That was Mr. Barker, the guy I interviewed with."

"I didn't like the way he stood over you."

I thought back to our conversation on the steps. "I don't remember him standing over me."

"Yeah, he was on the upper step, leaning down talking to you."

"Was he? I was about to walk away when he remembered to tell me about where the employees park. That's all he was doing."

"Maybe."

Mark started up the engine, pulled the car out of the parking spot, and headed for home.

My thoughts were swirling around the fact that we would finally have some income coming in. If Mark could just land another job, we'd be able to crawl out of this temporary dark hole we had sunk into.

Why did I not hear the jealousy creeping into Mark's psyche? Maybe because I had already mailed the letter turning down the job in Columbus. Maybe because I still believed that Mark had learned his lesson and would not act on his thoughts again. Maybe because I believed that I was the one woman he needed, the one who would help him through the problems his past had made him a victim of.

Or, maybe it was just old-fashioned, blind love.

Chapter 25

DON'T ACT RIGHT

While looking forward to receiving the job offer letter, I continued to walk to the pay phone daily to check for any other responses. Other than my parents' occasional calls, there were no other messages.

I knew that the new employer would probably check my references with my former Atlanta manager. Luke would be disappointed that I didn't come back but, other than that, I was sure the references would be good.

I waited longer than expected for the letter. Perhaps my former manager was more than disappointed. Perhaps he told Mr. Barker about my marriage situation and abrupt departure.

I went out to the pay phone three weeks later and had a message from an unfamiliar name with an unfamiliar phone number. The message did not say if the caller was from a company, but I had only given that number out on my resumes. It had to be in response to one of them, so I stayed at the phone booth and returned the call immediately.

"Rhonda Jacobs," a voice answered with a deep Southern drawl. Still no identification of the company.

"Hello, Rhonda. This is Maria Towns returning your phone call from earlier today."

"Yes, Maria. We were wondering why you didn't come in today?"

"Come in? Come in where?"

"Come in to work." She sounded just as confused as I was. "Today was your start date."

"Start date?"

"Yes. You were supposed to start today at 8 a.m."

I asked her what company she was with, and it was the same company where I had interviewed with Mr. Barker.

"Rhonda, I'm confused. I never got an offer letter. Mr. Barker said I would get one with a start date and all the other information, but I didn't get one..... I was thinking he had changed his mind."

"Well, I don't know anything about the offer letter and all that. I'll have to check with Mr. Barker."

"OK. Thank you for calling."

I hung up and walked back to the apartment, still confused about the call. I was sure we didn't discuss a definite start date. And what happened to the offer letter that I was promised?

I told Mark about the phone call and asked if he ever picked up an offer letter from the mail. He said that he had not. The longer I thought about it, the more I knew that he had. Mark was beginning to let jealous thoughts get in the way of good sense. He had gone so far as to sabotage my only job offer!

I needed to somehow get him into therapy.

Chapter 26

FOOL'S GOLD

BEING WITHOUT JOBS MEANT THAT we stayed up later and later each night. Sometimes we read books or played board games until 2 or 3 a.m. These activities created a cycle that I knew was not good. We awakened later and later each morning. Any job searches by Mark were being pushed into late afternoon.

Mark always wanted jobs where he could serve the black community, even though he didn't have a college degree.

"Mark," I said, "I know you want a community service job, but we need some income. For now, you're going to have to start looking for nonprofessional jobs. We cannot make it like this."

"I am not just looking for one type of job. I went out yesterday and applied for a job loading the airplanes."

I looked at Mark with a new appreciation, as I had not realized that he was ready to do manual labor. "Well, I'm glad of that, but you can't stop with just that one inquiry."

I sat across from him at the dining table. I decided to go a little further and tell him about my dream. I have always felt that dreams revealed some of our deepest fears and hopes.

"I had a dream last night," I said.

"Yeah?" He lit a cigarette.

"Yeah. I dreamed that you were driving the car by a big lake. You were driving too fast. The car kept swerving dangerously close to the lake."

He looked at me when I hesitated.

I went on. "Then all of a sudden the car veered into the lake. Instead of sinking, it skimmed the water until it made it over to the other side."

He chuckled. "Just goes to show you that I won't let you drown. I will steer us safely through."

I pressed my lips together and said nothing more. That was definitely not how I had interpreted the dream. I had interpreted it that we were on the verge of drowning, all because of Mark's recklessness.

Another bad side effect of having no jobs for either of us was that Mark's imagination was starting to get fertile again.

A week later, after Mark returned home from being out a while, he asked what I had been doing in his absence.

"Oh, let's see....I cleaned out a closet, and I watched a movie on TV. In fact, the movie was really interesting!"

I had enjoyed the movie tremendously, so I sat on the bed and launched into details of the storyline for Mark. He listened, but the more he listened, the more his lips tightened and the more pronounced his cheek bones became.

When I finished, he said, "You are so used to writing stories that you just make up stories as you go."

I was puzzled by his comment because, although I enjoyed writing, I hadn't written *any* stories since we had met. And, gosh, did he really think I could write something with as good a plot as the movie I had just watched? If so, I was in the wrong profession.

Later that evening, I realized that I had forgotten to tell Mark about one of my activities in his absence....I had washed my hair. I was actually drying it while I watched the movie. Mark was probably calculating that my activities didn't quite add up to the two hours he had been away.

I thought about telling him of my hair-washing activity, but then I decided against it. He really shouldn't have to know minute-by-minute details of my time alone. He was supposed to be on a non-jealous track, and I didn't need to supply that type of information.

One thing we did need was money. We were about to be evicted.

Chapter 27

EMOTIONAL ROLLERCOASTER

As expected, Mark's bad credit prevented him from getting another apartment. My credit was in real danger of going bad, but I thought perhaps I could get an apartment before my credit files got updated with the bills that I couldn't pay after I got back from Columbus.

I applied for a townhouse in another part of East Point. I told them that I had been staying with a friend since I moved out of my Campbellton Road apartment. My payment history for that apartment was good. I also put on my application that I was self-employed, doing temporary programming assignments. Within a couple of days, the answering service had a message that I was approved for the apartment.

Mark begged his family members for the money for a security deposit and the first month's rent. I applied for telephone service at the new apartment in my name. I had a good record for paying for the telephone at my previous apartment, so it was no problem to get the phone service transferred to my new location without a deposit.

A couple of days before the eviction orders came through, we moved into a nice, white brick townhouse with two bedrooms upstairs, and the living room, dining room, and kitchen downstairs. Every room except the kitchen had brown shag carpet as the flooring.

The only problem was that pets were not allowed. Mark's sister agreed to keep Leta and Hasana for a few months. Mark and I believed that once we got situated with jobs again, we could rent a small house and get the dogs back. I missed them greatly, and I hoped we could all be reunited soon.

I updated my parents with our new address and phone number.

We were starting anew—a new beginning. We just needed jobs to keep it going.

The week before Christmas in 1973, Mama called with the sad news that Muz had died.

Knowing our job situation, my parents volunteered to pay for my plane ticket to come home. I was only in Columbus a couple of days for the funeral, and then it was back to Atlanta again. I assured my parents that everything was going well with Mark. To me, "going well" meant that Mark was not hitting me.

For the first time since my pre-teen years, I wouldn't be able to buy any Christmas presents for my parents or my brother, but they said they understood. They gave me money for my Christmas gift. Yet Mark and I still desperately needed money.

We were getting the new apartment in shape. Mark's brothers came over and helped us move my bedroom suite out of storage and up to the second floor bedroom. Our living room was now a little more cramped because we had to put the record player, its stand, and all of our albums in it. We also put the extra TV and stand in the living room.

I sent out more resumes, hoping that some other companies would be interested in hiring me. At this point, we needed an infusion of money, and I was really ready for a full-time, permanent job.

My family and I had celebrated New Year's Eve for years by

going to church at 10 p.m. for Watch Meeting. Watch Meeting was a tradition stemming from the Emancipation Proclamation. In many places, blacks gathered in their churches on the last hour of December 31, 1862, and got on their knees to wait for midnight, the official end of slavery in the U.S. In our modern version of Watch Meeting, we would have a testimony period, hear a sermon, and then start praying on our knees a few minutes before midnight. Because of this tradition, I had never attended a New Year's Eve party.

Somehow Mark had enough money to bring home a bottle of red wine on December 31, 1973. At the stroke of midnight, we lifted up our wine glasses for a toast and we kissed. I leaned back on the sofa, smiling as I sipped the chilled sweet wine and watched the TV screen showing the ball dropping in New York.

This was new to me, but I liked it. I was full of hope that the year 1974 would be a year of love, Mark's healing, and jobs for us. Little did I know what was really in store for me in the new year.

1974

Chapter 28

THE REMIX

One cool January afternoon, after I vacuumed our shag carpet, I saw Mark lean over and stare intently at a spot on the living room floor. He pulled up a thin, one-inch-long fragment of paper from the carpet. Pushing the paper—a joint wrapper—toward my face, he said, "You've had a man in here smoking some weed!"

"No, I haven't!"

"Then how did this get here?"

"It's probably from one of your joints."

"I never use this color of wrapper."

Now it was my turn to stare at the paper. He was right! This was a white wrapper—a totally different color from the pale yellow wrappers he usually used.

I had no answer for him. I had just vacuumed, so how did that partial joint paper get there? Mark grunted "Mm-Hm" but, fortunately, he did not pursue this accusation.

A few days later, I was doing some additional cleaning in the apartment, and I found myself looking at any speck anywhere, trying to see if it was a joint wrapper. *Wait!* I asked myself, *Why am I looking for joints? I know I haven't had anybody in this apartment.*

Mark's delusions had made me start looking for any evidence that might point to something I hadn't done!

Mark needed those therapy sessions, but with neither one of us working, we couldn't afford them. I prayed for some employment... for both of us.

By the third week of January, we had an almost empty refrigerator and a few cans of food in the cabinets. To add to our problems, the phone started malfunctioning, so we couldn't dial out. Mark went to a nearby pay phone booth and called for repair service.

When he returned to the house, he said, "They'll be out Monday at 3 to repair the phone."

"Really?" I asked.

He chuckled. "Yeah. What did you expect?"

"Well, we are weeks behind with paying the phone bill. I was thinking they might not agree to fix the problem until we pay up."

"No," he scoffed. "They'd better not come up with any stuff like that."

On Monday, Mark left before 3 p.m. The telephone repairman showed up on time, fixed the problem, and left shortly after.

Mark came in an hour later with a small bag of groceries.

"It's not much, but at least it's some food." He opened the bag and pulled out an onion, a bag of rice, and a package of chicken livers. I really hated chicken livers, but we had no other meat. I was determined not to be down in the dumps; positivity was the order of the day.

I put the items in the refrigerator and followed Mark into the living room.

"Oh!" I said brightly, "The telephone repairman came, and the phone is working again."

Mark's tone turned somber. "When did he come?"

"Um, about an hour ago."

"What did he look like?"

"Oh, just an average looking white guy. I didn't pay a whole lot of attention to how he looked."

"Why was it he waited until I left?" Mark didn't even wait for an answer before he said, "Did he have a beard?"

I had to think about it. By now, I was mildly agitated. *If Mark was going to be this concerned about the man's appearance, why didn't he stick around until the appointment time?*

"Yes, he had a beard."

"What color was his hair?" Mark asked the question as he walked over to the record player and turned it on. He pulled a large, black LP from its album cover and placed the record on the player. He lifted the spindle from its resting place and lowered it onto the edge of the record.

I watched Mark's actions as I answered his question. "I don't know. I think he had dark hair."

Mark cranked the record player's volume up, much too loudly. *Why on earth would Mark turn up the volume like that? This doesn't mean he is planning to attack me, does it? Is this a setup like when he drove to a deserted area just before hitting me in the car? Or when he put the dogs away before choking me? Things have been going fairly well, and Mark has not hit me during all the time I've been back. Is he really going to break his promise? Was it all a big lie? Lord, I don't want to fight.*

Mark did want to fight. He rammed me.

With his fist. In my face.

"Unh!" I reached up my hands to grab my face.

In my stomach.

I lowered my hands to protect my stomach.

In my temple.

My hands couldn't fly fast enough to cover all the places he was hitting me. I tried hitting back, but each time I did, he blocked my moves and hammered whatever part of my body wasn't protected. It seemed as though he got angrier and more forceful with every punch.

His fists were pummeling me over and over again, while he accused me of doing all types of things with this repairman whose name I didn't even know.

He leaped up and bulldozed me with a karate kick in my stomach. I wobbled like a boxer losing the fight, almost unable to keep my balance. My hands didn't fly up so fast anymore to protect myself from his blows. The metallic taste of blood crept into my mouth.

A midnight fog was closing in, trying to block out my eyesight. Now my battle was against that fog. It would have been so easy to just dissolve into the fog. The physical pain of each new punch would go away. The pain of knowing that Mark had lied would go away.

But no, he might just keep beating me and then I would die. There would be no bell or referee to eventually save me from the torture.

He kept ramming his fists all over me, as I stumbled around trying to stay upright and fighting against the fog. I had no idea of the timing of this beating. Through the haze and the pain, my mind was focused on how to survive.

I was losing in this battle to resist his fists and stay on my feet. In desperation, I let out a yell like a two-year-old having a temper tantrum.

"YEEEHHHNNNN!" I howled as I lashed out at the blaring record player and yanked it onto the floor. The loud music abruptly became the sound of a quick r-r-r-rip. The ripping sound exploded into a loud crash.

And then there was total silence.

Chapter 29

END OF THE ROAD

Mark finally stopped hitting me. His arms fell to his sides, as he looked down at the record player whose spindle lay limply at an angle on the crooked turntable. Still staring down at the catastrophe on the floor, he weakly asked, "Why did you do that?"

I thought he would become angrier at my destruction of the record player. Instead, he gingerly picked up the record player and set it back on its stand.

He lifted up the cracked, big, black LP record that had been playing. After inspecting it, he laid it off to the side of the record player. Then he turned and looked at me for a second, confusion and hurt in his eyes.

Abruptly, he walked into the kitchen. In the meantime, I stumbled over to the bottom of the steps and sat down. Every piece of my battered body was an ache. I leaned my elbows on my knees and propped my throbbing head up with both hands.

When Mark came back from the kitchen, his eyes smoldered like burning coals. But they weren't as scary as the large butcher knife which he grasped in his right hand. The way I felt then, he could have plunged that knife into my heart and I wouldn't have tried to stop him. I was ready to give into the fog, the knife, whatever…. that's how weakened and tired of the beating I was.

His angry voice had returned like clashing cymbals in search of an orchestra. He sat down beside me on the steps and laid the knife between us.

He was talking to me; yet my mind was not absorbing many of the words he was saying. I understood him, though, when he said, "I should kill you now!" In my aching head, I wanted this all to be over. I no longer saw survival in my future; therefore, I silently waited for him to go ahead and end my life.

Suddenly he yelled, "Get out! Just *get out*!"

I couldn't believe that I was going to get through this alive! I was unable to move at my normal speed, so I made my way slowly to the closet and pulled my heaviest coat out.

I had to steady myself against the wood frame of the closet door in order to get both arms into the coat but, finally, I had it on. I pulled my purse down from the closet shelf as a burning pain shot through my torso. Then I walked carefully to the front door.

Mark just watched me as he remained on the steps. I had no energy left in my body, but I was free!

I took a few steps and opened the door, not knowing where I would go, or if I could even make it to the end of the long sidewalk leading out to the parking lot.

Slowly, I walked down the short stairwell of our townhouse stoop, leaning heavily on the railing in order to keep myself upright. I needed to turn loose and somehow walk down the sidewalk completely on my own strength. Could I do it?

I tried to recharge myself with the realization that I was free from Mark. *I think I have a dime. If I can make it to a pay phone booth, I can call my cousin Lena. She will come and get me. But where is the nearest phone booth?*

I took one step.

Lena will be shocked at how I look. She won't believe that this was the work of the mild-mannered man I had introduced to her and her husband.

I took another step, not knowing how long I could stay up straight.

It doesn't matter what anybody thinks. It just matters that I get away.

I took one more step.

"Maria!" It was Mark's voice calling me.

Chapter 30

FATHER, I STRETCH MY HANDS TO THEE

"Come on back in here!" Mark said in disgust.

I looked over my shoulder and saw him standing at the open door of the apartment. My head jerked back toward the parking lot. I wanted with all my heart to take off running away from him.

The parking lot was right there, just past three more townhouses, but that night the distance loomed longer than the length of a football field. I had no strength to walk to the end of the sidewalk, let alone to run. And I knew Mark would quickly overtake me either way. I turned around and weakly made the three steps back to the townhouse.

Once inside, Mark pointed his chin toward the staircase. "Go to the bathroom and clean yourself up."

It was a long slow haul but, finally, I made it up the steps to the bathroom. That was when I looked in the mirror and saw how awful I looked.

Blood splatter covered my blouse. I had fresh red bruises all around both eyes. One eye was on the verge of swelling shut. My short Afro was matted down with sweat.

My nose was running, causing snot to mingle with the blood

coming from my nose. I couldn't stand up straight because of the pain in my torso. I just leaned on the sink and ran cold water over my face with one hand, but nothing could rinse away the ugliness of the whole experience.

Mark had followed me up the steps and he started fussing again. He was still an angry man, but his talk was more subdued. He was in the bedroom while I was cleaning up in the bathroom.

At some point during his rant, still implying that I had done something wrong, he said, "You must think I'm crazy.....!"

I had been reeling with the thought that this evening was something straight out of a psychology textbook, where a personality just takes an opposite turn. I said very softly, "You are."

"I heard that!" he said sharply. I don't think he heard exactly what I said because he stayed in the bedroom.

After he figured I'd been in the bathroom long enough, he ordered me to get ready for bed. My sore body felt like a china pot that had been cracked all over. One flick of a finger against the pot would make the whole thing tinkle into a glassy pile.

Carefully and slowly, I got my night clothes on and crawled into the bed. I turned toward the wall, away from a now-silent Mark who followed me into the bed. My body couldn't run, but my mind was running in its place. The only thought repeatedly going through my head: *If I ever get away from him, I'm never coming back!*

Then Mark scooted close and touched the hem of my gown. My body stiffened at his touch. I felt him raise the gown upward until his fingers touched my underwear. I stopped breathing. "No," my inner voice groaned, as he pulled down my underwear.

He was aroused, and he pushed his body closer to mine. I felt a sour fullness swelling up from my insides trying to get into my mouth. It wanted to come all the way out of me. With every bit of strength I had left, I fought to keep it down. I didn't want Mark to have any reason to get angry again.

Mark turned my aching body—full of large, purple-red

bruises—toward him, and he immediately started having sex with me. I squeezed my eyes shut as tight as I could to stop the briny tears from coming out of them. Still, one stream of wetness rolled down toward my ear and settled there. Instead of thinking about what was happening to me, my mind kept pleading a simple prayer to God: *Lord, if you let me get away...*

Chapter 31

GOD IS REAL

The next day Mark acted as if nothing unusual had happened. The only difference was he wouldn't leave the house. I'm sure he was thinking about how I left the last time, and he was not going to give me an opportunity to flee.

My face was more swollen than it was the night before. The bruises around my eyes were turning dark blue. I had no desire to go out in public, but if I could get away....

All we had in the refrigerator were the items Mark had brought from the grocery store the previous day and an orange. I did not want chicken livers but, if I was going to eat that day, then chicken livers it would be.

I was a big dessert person. If I had no dessert, I would bake something. I always felt prosperous when I had dessert and, for that reason, I tried to ensure there was always sugar, flour, milk, butter, and eggs in the kitchen. That day, none of those things was there.

I was grateful for the one orange in the fruit bin. I sat at the eating bar, peeling that orange and telling myself this sweet, juicy fruit would be my dessert.

As I was finishing up the orange, the phone rang, and Mark answered it.

"Oh, hi, Mrs. Jordan."

I quickly looked up. Was this my mother calling? Mark was looking in wonderment at me as he talked happily.

"Good. Yes, I'm doing fine! How are you doing?"

He paused for her answer.

"Sure, she's here. Just a minute," he said before handing the phone to me.

I was elated, but how could I possibly let her know what was going on? Mark stood right there by the phone, watching and listening to what I would say.

We exchanged pleasantries, and then my mother said, "Well, I'm calling to let you know that Dad and Richard left this morning on their way to Atlanta."

I caught my breath. *Is this real? How did they know I was in trouble?*

She went on. "They are going to spend tonight in Louisville, so they should arrive in Atlanta sometime late tomorrow afternoon."

Help was on the way! Ah, Perfect God, I surely didn't expect my rescue to come this quickly and this definitively. Thank you, Jesus!! That was my internal reaction.

Externally, I tried to sound nonchalant. "Oh, really? What is the occasion?" I wouldn't look at Mark for fear that he would see the relief that must have brightened my face at that point. I did a half-turn in my chair, away from him.

"Well, you know Dad mentioned to you that he wanted to work with Mark and others in Atlanta to start up a school like the job training school here. He just made the decision to do it this week while Richard was out of school for winter break. That way Richard could drive him there."

"Oh, I see."

My mother and I went on casually chatting a few more minutes, but my mind was busy with plans for my getaway. *My father and brother are going to have a fit when they see what I look like! I have to figure out how to get them to just take me back to Columbus without wasting time getting angry with Mark.*

Our conversation had ended, and I hung up the phone before turning back to Mark.

"What's up?" Mark asked.

"She called to tell me that my father and brother are on their way to Atlanta." I tried hard to make it sound like I was just saying something normal, like "It's raining outside."

"What? Did you call them?"

"No." I wondered when Mark thought I would have called. Except for when I went to the bathroom, he had not let me out of his sight since the previous night. "My father wants you to introduce him to all the right people in Atlanta who can help fund the training school. You know, he's mentioned that to you several times."

He quickly dispensed the reason for the visit. "How are we going to explain how you look?" he asked.

"I don't know."

In my mind I thought, *Now it's "we" who have to explain how I look! "We" didn't do this to me!*

What I said out loud after thinking a few moments was, "Well, they know we just moved into a new apartment and that we had to move furniture around…"

"Yeah?" he said, as though he wanted me to say more.

"I suppose we could say that we were moving something heavy—like the dresser—upstairs. And I slipped and the dresser fell back on me."

I doubt they will believe this story, knowing Mark's past history. But at this point, I don't really care. I will be safe once they get here and I can get away! I need to stay safe until that time.

"Well, what do you think they'll say about the injuries?" he asked me.

I wanted to say, *They'll probably bash your head in*, but I knew that wasn't the thing to say right then.

I thought a few seconds and said, "They'll probably ask me if I've been to the hospital."

"You think so? Well, we'd better get you to the hospital tonight so we can say 'yes' to that question."

"We don't have any insurance, Mark."

"That doesn't matter. We'll go to Grady Memorial. They take you whether or not you have insurance."

I rummaged through my old purses and found a pair of sunglasses. I put them on to try to cover up the damage to my face, but the blue and purple bruises were like a huge mask, much larger than the area covered by the glasses.

While driving me to the hospital, Mark said, "Now that's the story we'll say at the hospital, too. The dresser fell back on you as we were moving it upstairs."

He was silent for another minute, then asked, "Are your father and brother planning to stay at our house, or are they staying in a hotel?"

"I don't know. My mother didn't say. We'll just have to figure that out when they get here."

I thought about the fact that we didn't have any food other than a few chicken livers. *Well, it doesn't much matter. I don't plan to spend another night with Mark once they get here. All I want them to do is get me out of here.*

Chapter 32

THIS MASQUERADE

After sitting in the hospital's crowded ER for three hours, a young doctor finally started examining me. Fortunately, he took me into a private room and left Mark out in the waiting area.

The doctor sat on his stool and looked at me seriously. "Now tell me how you got these bruises?"

"We were moving a dresser up the stairs, and I slipped and the dresser fell back on me."

The doctor locked his eyes straight on mine, folded his arms, and slowly shook his head from side to side. "Those types of bruises aren't consistent with that kind of accident."

I was weary and not stuck on holding onto that tale. All I really wanted to do was to stay alive until my father and brother got there.

"OK. I'll tell you what really happened, but don't let my husband know that I told you the true story."

The doctor nodded his agreement. I gave him the real story.

"Alright." He leaned forward, carefully touching my face. "These facial bruises look pretty serious. I want to get you up to x-ray." He stood up to leave, but stopped suddenly.

"I won't say anything to your husband, but you do know that beatings like this can kill you, don't you?"

"Yes," I said softly as I lowered my eyes to the floor. I needed to let the doctor know that I wasn't planning to meekly settle for this lifestyle anymore. I lifted up my eyes and looked straight at him.

"This was my husband's second chance to save our marriage," I said with a sigh. "I know now that he cannot change. My father is on his way to Atlanta now. When he gets here, I am leaving my husband, leaving this town, and I'm never coming back."

He patted my shoulder. "OK. I'll see you after we get these x-rays. I'll tell your husband he can come in now."

Mark came into the room.

"The doctor said they are sending you to x-ray."

"Yes."

A nurse was coming in the room, pushing a wheelchair right behind him.

"Mrs. Towns, we're going to take you up to x-ray now. Let me help you into this wheelchair, and we'll get you right up there."

She held me on one side, and Mark held me on the other side. I had walked into ER on my own power, but now I was being treated as though I could no longer do that.

There were the usual hours of ER waiting. Waiting for the x-ray technician. Going to another exam room and waiting for the doctor to look at the x-rays so he could come and talk to me.

Finally, the young doctor did reappear, and he talked to us as if he were talking to a normal married couple.

"The x-rays show that you have a broken bone in your left jaw, right under your eye. You will have to get that repaired."

I frowned deeply at the realization that Mark had actually broken one of my bones. I could remember distinctly when he landed that punch under my eye, because I had hollered and grabbed that part of my face with both hands.

The doctor went on. "We will keep you overnight so the surgeons can take a look at the x-rays in the morning and tell you exactly how that can be surgically repaired."

I let out a surprised gasp because I certainly had not planned to stay in the hospital.

"We are getting a room ready for you, but it may take a while since this was unexpected on our end."

"OK," I mumbled.

Mark looked just as dumbfounded as I did. He put his arm around my waist. "I'm sure it will be alright. We'll see what the doctors say in the morning."

"Yes."

"We'll have you good as new in no time," Mark said as he kissed a bruise on my cheek.

We waited in the examining room for about an hour. We read the two or three magazines that they had in the room. We talked about his family news, why hospital ERs always involve a long wait, what was going on with Nixon and the Watergate tapes, and how Leta and Hasana were doing. But we never talked about what he did that led to us being in that examining room.

Finally, we were taken to the hospital room where I was given a hospital gown with its typical backside opening. It was a big room, especially considering that there was only one bed in there. It also had two white chairs for visitors and a small, white nightstand. Oddly enough, there was no phone and TV.

I changed into the gown, then climbed into the bed so that the nurses in their starched white uniforms and caps could begin recording my vitals. Mark cheerfully chatted with each person who came into the room. Between their appearances, he kept talking to me about everything except his Big Lie. It had gotten to be 11:00 p.m., and I was fearful that he was going to spend the night in that chair by my bed.

Eventually, he said, "Is it okay for me to go back to the apartment and get some sleep?"

"Sure."

He kissed me on the forehead. "I'll see you in the morning."

"OK."

I wondered if he realized that I hadn't asked him to bring my gown, robe, or slippers from the house. I waited until he had been gone about 30 minutes. Then, just to be sure, I decided to wait another five minutes.

It was late, but I had important things to take care of. I got out of the bed and eased into my white tennis shoes. Wrapping the back of my hospital gown around me as best I could, I headed down the hall toward the nurses' station. A solitary nurse was sitting there, writing on some papers.

"I need to make a long-distance call," I said. "Where can I do that?"

"Is it a collect call?"

"Yes."

"Oh well, you can do that here." She produced a phone from under the desk ledge and set it on the counter for me.

"Thank you so much!"

I dialed the number for my mother. Once we got through the preliminaries of her accepting the collect call, I began speaking. I knew she would wonder why I was calling her so late.

"Mom, I'm in the hospital—"

"What for?"

"Mark beat me last night." I didn't wait for her reaction because time was important. "This one was so bad that he broke my jaw bone. I am leaving him for good, but here's what I need you to do. Can you get in touch with Dad and Richard in Louisville? Do you know who they are staying with?"

"I'm not sure which relative they were going to, but I will try to find them."

"Can you please call them and explain what happened? But tell them to just be cool and go along with the story."

"What story?"

"We are saying that I got hurt moving furniture up the stairs.

But I figure they won't believe that, and I don't want to waste time with them getting angry. All I want them to do is to get me out of here and back to Columbus."

"OK. I can do that, but what are the doctors saying about your broken bone?"

"I need surgery for that. They will tell me more in the morning. But I don't want to wait for the surgery. I want to leave."

"Alright. I'll try to find them. Are you safe right now?"

"Yes. I'm safe. Mark has gone back to the apartment for the night. And I know he won't hurt me when they are here. I just want to go home."

I said goodbye, thanked the nurse for letting me use the phone, and toddled back to my room. I prayed that my father and brother had stayed with one of our relatives in Louisville and that my mother would be able to find them. Then I drifted off to sleep, aided by the pain medicines they had given me.

Chapter 33

LESSON LEARNED

MARK ARRIVED IN MY ROOM early the next morning, dressed in his usual sports jacket, shirt, and tie. I had already awakened and taken my shower.

"How did you sleep last night?" he asked.

"Pretty well. You know how it is in a hospital. Someone comes in your room several times during the night to check on something or other."

"Yeah." He smiled as he sat in the chair by my bed. "Do you need anything?"

"No. They already told me that I was on a no-solid food diet, so when my breakfast comes, it will just be oatmeal and tea."

"That's more than what I had this morning." Mark gave a short laugh. "Do you know what time your father is coming in?"

"No, I don't. They'll be driving from Louisville this morning, so I'd guess they would leave at 7 or later. I don't remember how long it takes to get from there to here."

"OK. I need to check on that."

Mark paused, then went on. "They finally turned our phone off for nonpayment, so I'll need to be at the house. Otherwise, they won't be able to reach me."

"They probably will just come on to the house without calling. They have the address, and they will have a map."

The door of my room opened just then, and three doctors walked in. The lead doctor was tall and thin, with graying hair. The other two might have been interns, but they both appeared to be in their 30s.

"Well, Mrs. Towns, we are going to have to go in and repair your broken jaw bone," said the older doctor after he introduced himself and asked how I felt. "What we'll do is put a rod in to hold the two broken pieces together and to keep your facial structure in place. We will have to attach a cork to the end of the rod. That will sit on the outside of your face, just at the side of your cheek."

"A cork?" I asked, frowning.

"How big is that cork?" Mark asked.

"About this size." The doctor spread his thumb and index finger about a half-inch apart.

"It won't exactly be pretty, but it's the only way we can hold that rod up right now."

I had never in life seen anyone walking around with a cork sticking out of the side of their cheek. You couldn't hide it with long straight hair, and you certainly couldn't hide it with an Afro. I didn't want to have a cork hanging on my face.

"What happens if I don't do the surgery?" I asked. Out of the corner of my eye, I could see Mark's head swing around and look at me.

"If you don't have the surgery within five days, that side of your face will begin to sink inward. You will always have a lopsided face as a result."

My breaths came quickly in short puffs. *This is what I am getting for sticking with Mark. For thinking that we could work through his sickness. I will be a strange sight for the rest of my life! An oddity!*

There were no tears, no hysterics. Instead, I bit my bottom lip and tried to resign myself to the fact that Mark had ruined me forever. Children would point at me and ask their parents questions. No man—not even a husband would want me again. *All because I stupidly decided to come back to him. This will be the last thing he does to me!*

I couldn't look at Mark. I just looked helplessly at the doctor.

"I know this is a lot to spring on you right now. Do you want some time to think about it, Mrs. Towns?" the doctor asked. "We can do the surgery in two to three days when some of the swelling goes down on your face."

"Yes, I need some time to process all this, please." I felt the frown deepening on my face.

"That's fine. We'll be back tomorrow to check out the swelling and to talk some more."

The doctors left the room, as I thought about this new development. *How can I possibly get to Columbus, see another doctor, and get the surgery done within five days?*

"You've got to get that surgery done, Maria!" Mark was pressing.

My throat was suddenly parched. I still didn't look at him. Instead, I poured a glass of water from the pitcher on the side table.

"I suppose. It's just something that I hadn't expected. Who wants to wear a cork on their face?"

"Well, who wants one side of their face sagging in?" Mark asked.

I drank the water, not believing Mark was saying that, since he was the cause of the whole problem. Still, my job was to keep the peace, stay safe, and get out of Atlanta. I gave no response as I slipped deep into thought.

If my father hadn't been on his way to Atlanta, Mark never would have taken me to the hospital, and I never would have known about the broken bone, and I eventually would have had a lopsided face. That isn't going to be my outcome. I need to count my blessings.

Mark had brought a newspaper to the hospital with him, so he spent time talking to me about what he had read in the paper. I decided I'd better keep going along with the happy husband/wife act.

He finally determined from one of the hospital workers how long it would take for someone to travel from Louisville to Atlanta by car. Meanwhile, the pain medicine caused me to periodically doze off.

I received a liquid lunch of tomato soup, vanilla pudding, apple juice, and tea. Since I disliked tomato soup, I gave that to Mark while I consumed the other items.

Mark stayed in the room until it was almost 3 p.m. Then he figured he needed to go wait for my father and brother at the house. I used that break to fully doze. I had not figured out the logistics of leaving Mark, but I knew my father would have some ideas.

Chapter 34

I AM CHANGING

"There she is!" Mark entered my hospital room, smiling broadly, a couple of hours later. Dad and Richard followed behind him.

I was just waking up and did not have my sunglasses on, so the blue-purple bruises all over my face were on full display.

"Mm-mm. Those are terrible bruises!" My father pulled over a chair so that he could sit down and face my bed. He adjusted his glasses on his nose and searched all over my face in deep concentration. "And the doctors say you've got a broken bone besides?"

"Yes." I was searching my father's face as well. "I've got to get surgery for it within five days or my face will be permanently sagged in."

Dad's brow had wrinkled more. I could not figure out if he knew the truth or if he was going on Mark's story. By now, my brother was leaning over and looking intently at my face. One side of his face twitched as though he were viewing something revolting. Indeed, it *was* revolting.

"Does it hurt much?" Richard asked.

"Well, they are giving me some pain medication, so it doesn't hurt much anymore."

"That's good 'cause it looks like it would hurt a lot otherwise." Richard looked at me a little longer with that pained expression 'on his face. Finally, he retreated to the only other chair, while Mark stood off to the side.

My father sometimes had a nervous tic where he would rapidly shake his right leg up and down while seated. That leg was shaking now as he still frowned at my face. He asked questions about the doctors, who they were and when they were returning. He got up slowly and walked out in the hall, looking for a nurse and more information.

When Dad felt he understood the situation, he came back to the room, tired and anxious to sit down again. He sat, just as he was consumed by a hacking cough that lasted for about a minute. We then talked about their plans for the evening. They had had a lengthy drive, and no business could be conducted today. Dad volunteered to go to a hotel and asked Mark to lead them to one so that they could rest for the night. After another few minutes of conversation, all three men headed out. Mark returned shortly and kept up his vigil at my bedside until about 10 p.m.

I resented him acting as though he cared, and I wanted him to go home. Outwardly, I kept up my act, as if he belonged there, that he was really a dutiful husband, and that things were just fine between us. I played the role well because I had a very firm goal of keeping the peace until I could leave Atlanta.

The next morning Mark showed up in my room early and alone again, wearing a tan sports jacket over dark brown pants. He brought the change of underwear that I had asked him for the previous night.

Smiling at me, he asked, "How did you sleep last night?"

"I slept very well between the nurses' visits."

"Good. I didn't stop by the hotel this morning. Your father said they would be able to get over here on their own."

He sat down and placed a book and newspaper on the nightstand.

"Have the doctors been back by?"

"No, I haven't seen them yet."

"What are you going to tell them? About the surgery?"

"Yeah, I'll have it," I said wearily.

"Good!" He nodded with satisfaction. "Hey, I came early because I've got to go to a short meeting at 9:30 am. Will you be okay with me being gone for an hour or so?"

Why, I wondered, *is he asking me that? Normally, he goes wherever he wants without asking what I think.*

I suppose I took too long to answer that question because he went on. "I'm really sorry about leaving you. This meeting was set up before I knew you'd be in the hospital and long before I knew your father would be here. After I get back, we can figure out whom he wants to talk to first about the training school."

"Yeah, it's okay."

Mark was still busy apologizing, but I was thinking that if my father could get here while Mark was out, I could find out how much he knew about the situation.

The hospital staff came in with the same liquid breakfast, which I shared with Mark since he said he had only had tea that morning. He pointed out the newspaper stories of interest to me between laughing and talking with the nurses and aides who came in.

I thought to myself, *He watched me like a hawk the day after he beat me. He's acting as if everything is just fine now. How is it that he doesn't realize I'm going to leave him and that it will be for good this time?*

At 9 o'clock, Mark apologized again for having to leave me and go to his meeting.

"Do you need me to bring you anything?"

"No." I wondered how he thought he could afford to bring me anything if I *did* need it. I then wondered how he was able to afford the newspapers he had brought in the past two days and the hospital parking fees.

About 45 minutes after Mark left, my father and brother came through the door. The shocker was that my mother followed behind them!

My mouth gaped open, and then I asked her, "How did you get here?"

She pressed her lips inward, while she came close and examined my face with her eyes. I had already looked at myself that morning in the small mirror in the room, so I knew what she was seeing.

Both my eyes had continued to swell. The right eye was swollen shut. A bloody veil partially hid the white of my left eye. The large swollen area around both eyes had ripened to a deep black-like, purple. Even though she didn't say it, I knew my mother's heart was broken to see her child looking like that.

Dad asked me if Mark was anywhere in the hospital. I shook my head. Then I asked my question again, "How did Mama get here?"

Dad said, "I called her last night and asked her to fly down here. There's no way Richard and I could have handled moving you out of here by ourselves. It would have all been on Richard to do everything. And you're not in any condition to drive your car all the way back to Columbus."

I finally let out a giant sigh of relief. *They are all mobilized to help me leave. Even though I made this foolish decision to return to Mark and even though I am suffering because of it, they are still ready to help me get out of this situation.*

"What did the doctors say today?" My mother asked as she gently turned my head with her fingers so that she could look at each bruise. As she did so, I smelled the comforting, spring-flower aroma of my mother's favorite body lotion.

"The doctors haven't been in today," I answered. So all I know is what they said yesterday. I need surgery within five days—now four days—for the broken jawbone. If I don't get it by then, that side of my face will start sagging. If I do get it, I'll be wearing a cork on my face—forever."

"Don't worry about that," Dad said quickly. "We can get all that fixed in Columbus."

"I don't have any insurance." My voice sounded like a tiny, repentant, disobedient child.

"Don't worry about that now," my father repeated.

My mother jumped in. "Are there bruises anywhere else?"

"He punched and kicked me in my stomach. It hurts there when I move certain ways."

"But no broken bones there?" she asked.

"They didn't find any there."

"OK." she said with finality. "Are you ready to go?"

I nodded.

"Do you have your apartment keys?" Mama had analyzed the situation and was ready to take action.

"Yes."

"Well, let's go. You'll need to check yourself out of the hospital."

I threw the covers back, gripped my hospital gown around my backside, and the two of us went up to the nurses' station.

"I am leaving the hospital now." I said to the nurse. "How do I get discharged?"

The nurse looked shocked. "Do you know this is against the advice of the doctors?"

"Yes," I answered.

"We'll be traveling," my mother piped in. "Can you get some pain medication for her to take?"

"Why—yes. She'll need to fill out some paperwork while I call for the medicine and a prescription."

I filled out all the necessary paperwork and moved as quickly as I could to get dressed, put my sunglasses back on, and leave the hospital before Mark's return.

We made a quick stop to a grocery store where my brother and mother picked up a few small boxes. It wasn't long before my family and I were pulling into my apartment's parking lot.

Mark was not there, as expected. We immediately went upstairs and emptied my clothes out of the closets, loading up my two suitcases.

I knew that, back in Columbus, I would stay with my parents until I got on my feet again. Therefore, I had no need for the bedroom suite that I brought into the marriage. Neither did I need any of my kitchen utensils or my TV trays or stools. Everything else in the apartment was Mark's.

My mother, my brother, and I moved to get all the clothes out as quickly as possible. Richard piled the extra clothes over the back seat of my father's car. The plan was to have Mama drive me in my car and have Richard drive my father in Dad's black Lincoln Continental. Since my mother had brought only a fold-over bag for her clothes, there would be plenty of room for my things in my car.

My father had two more coughing fits, so he seated himself on the living room sofa, unable to help in the packing effort. Mama and I were still pulling clothes out of closets and drawers upstairs when I heard Mark's panicked voice downstairs. My heart rate immediately quickened, but I remembered that Mark probably wouldn't harm me with my family there.

Chapter 35

STAND

"Rev. Jordan, sir! Where's Maria?" Mark asked. Obviously, he was returning from the hospital where he discovered that I had checked out.

I assumed that my father pointed toward the stairs because the next thing I heard was the sound of Mark's footsteps racing up to the bedroom.

The surprise of seeing my mother showed in his eyes.

"Mrs. Jordan," he said in quiet acknowledgment.

My mother folded her arms across her chest and looked at him with both corners of her mouth turned down. She silently gave him a single nod of the head.

Mark turned to me.

"Can I talk to you, Maria?"

"I don't have time for talk now, Mark." I piled another drawer full of clothes into a corrugated, brown box.

"Just for two minutes," he pleaded.

"I'll give you one minute only."

"Alright."

He looked at my mother, but she had planted her feet like a

centurion guard. She had no plans to leave the room, and I had no plans for her to leave either.

Mark looked back at me. "I know you're planning to leave me, but I want you to stay." He then added emphatically, "I am *so sorry* for all the hurt and pain I caused you. I need you, Maria."

I let out a long breath. *What kind of man is this anyway? He has been with me for three whole days and has never once said that he was sorry for what he did to me. It doesn't matter. He is a liar.*

"Yes, I am leaving. We tried it a second time, and this is what I got for it!" I yanked my sunglasses off my face to expose those hideous, dark purple bruises again. "That's not the way you show love."

He winced. "I know that now. I love you—deeply." He placed his fisted arm across his heart and pumped it there. "You're my queen! The love of my life! Can't you see that?"

"No," I said quietly, putting the sunglasses back on. "I can't see that."

My mother unfolded her arms and hurried to put the rest of my underclothes in the boxes on the bed. Meanwhile, my brother had come upstairs to get the remaining boxes.

"We're through here," I told Richard. Carrying boxes of clothes, we all headed downstairs in single file--everyone but Mark.

"Dad, we're ready to go," I said as we reached the living room.

Mark had walked downstairs and over toward my father, who was still sitting on the sofa.

"Rev. Jordan, I'm really sorry about all this. I love Maria. I didn't mean to hurt her." His voice had begun breaking.

My father just shook his head slowly. The emphysema and the rush of that morning caused him to be out of breath, but he was determined to say one last thing to Mark. "When Maria was a girl, we only had to spank her once about anything...... She doesn't like to disappoint..... *IF* she had been doing something wrong as a wife,....she would have gotten it and corrected it immediately."

He looked up at Mark with an owlish look he had reserved for any young man who dared to visit me at my house during my teen years. "Besides, *nothing…absolutely nothing…*that any woman does…calls for what you did to Maria!" Then Dad slowly pushed himself up from the couch so that he could leave a final word of wisdom.

"Son," he said as he stood and stabbed a finger at him in the air, "you need to get some help."

I headed over toward Mark as he hung his head at this admonition. "I need my car keys," I said. He dug into his pocket for them and dropped them into my outstretched hand. I said nothing else as I turned toward the door and handed the keys to Mama.

Richard had been standing by the door, but he suddenly walked to the center of the room where Mark was standing. Instead of staying upset with him, he was overwhelmed by Mark's crushed paper-bag look. Mark's eyebrows formed a wrinkled line over both eyes, and his usually erect shoulders were drooping.

Even as an 18-year-old, Richard saw that this man's world had folded in on him, providing him with no clue on how to emerge from the mess. Richard adjusted the box he was carrying so he could reach down and pull up Mark's limp hand. Shaking it, he said simply, "You're still my brother-in-law."

I frowned and stuck out my lower lip in disagreement, but said nothing. Just before I turned away to head out the door, the tears that had dammed behind Mark's glasses quietly glistened down both sides of his face.

My family and I made our way down the long sidewalk to the parking lot. The shift during that walk was like Dorothy and Toto emerging from the terrifying, sepia-toned tornado episode into the Technicolor Land of Oz. We were on beautiful ground!

At last, I could appreciate the warmth and sunniness of that January day. We were coatless because the temperature was in the

70s. This was a weather anomaly, even for Atlanta, but still it was a gorgeous day! It signaled the first new beginning since I'd met Mark.

My mother slid into the driver's side of my car, and I sat down on the passenger's side. I slowly exhaled while leaning back against the seat. As Mama followed Dad's car through the streets of Atlanta, I turned my face toward the open window and drank in the warm air rushing against it.

The car whizzed past tall bare trees that seemed as bleak as my bruised condition and the doctor's diagnosis; yet my sense of freedom was like a bird soaring up to the tallest tree.

Chapter 36

I WILL SURVIVE

Back in Columbus, my father arranged for me to get the needed surgery within the required time limit. I did not know how he managed that until I got a call from Admissions while I was recovering from surgery in Mount Carmel East Hospital. Based on their questions and comments, I realized that I had been admitted as a welfare patient.

Nobody in my family had ever been on welfare. We all worked: as cooks, maids, sanitation workers, secretaries, small business owners, whatever. I felt that my being in this position was a slap in the face to every grandparent, aunt, and uncle who had encouraged me by sending some of their hard-earned dollars while I was in college. They had put their hopes and dreams into a better life for me. Now, my decisions alone had led me to be in this state.

A nurse came into my room later that afternoon. She had previously made special efforts to befriend me, and I had confided in her my story of abuse.

"Do you need anything, hon?" she asked.

"No, I'm fine. Thank you."

"Was that your husband who called you this morning?"

Confused, I shook my head.

"Oh," she went on, "you were awfully upset when I came through the room this morning. You were hanging up the phone, so I just assumed it was him bothering you."

I thought back to the calls I had received from my parents that morning. Then I remembered the call from the Admissions office. Evidently, my disgust at the welfare situation had shown on my face. I had been so upset that I didn't remember seeing this nurse in my room then.

"Um. No, that was something else." I finally said.

"You still having nightmares when you try to sleep?" she asked.

"Yes," I sighed. "It's always the same thing. Some people that I don't even know come into the room and start beating me up for no reason at all."

She patted my arm. "Just give it time. Those nightmares will go away eventually."

I nodded.

Little did I know that bigger concerns than nightmares and welfare were about to stalk our family. My mother went into the hospital a couple of weeks after I came out.

I refused to believe it when Dad told us the doctors diagnosed her with terminal cancer. Then Mom tried to hand me instructions for what to do after her death. I told her that we didn't need them. I totally rejected the thought that I could lose my mother.

Meanwhile, Mark somehow got access to phone service again, and he was relentless in calling.

One night, I lay on my bed listening to the "Blue Monday" broadcast on our local R & B radio station. *"Ain't No Way"*, a mournful, yet sweet song by Aretha Franklin was playing. That had been one of my favorite songs when I was in college. But I had mistakenly thought it was about a woman who failed to win a man's love. I frowned as I listened to the lyrics this particular evening because I finally heard its real message. Aretha was singing about a man whose *actions* kept her from loving him, even though she really wanted to. It amazed me that I didn't hear that until I was in a similar situation!

The phone rang, and I was surprised to hear Mrs. Towns' cheerful voice when I picked it up. After a few pleasantries and an inquiry about my health, she said, "I want you to know that you can come back. You won't be alone. We will all be here for you."

I wanted to laugh in her ear, but since I respect my elders and I still had respect for her, I just listened and then ended by calmly saying, "No, Mrs. Towns, I won't be coming back. But I do appreciate your calling to check on me." Once I hung up the phone, my hand rested on the handset while I softly sighed to myself, "Ain't no way."

Next, Mark had Sheila call and ask me to come back. Sheila was the former civil rights activist who had given the speech about staying in contact with prisoners.

"Sheila, did Mark tell you why I left?" I asked after she made her plea.

"No," she answered.

I provided her with all the details of Mark's abuse.

At the end, I said, "Sheila, my hearing has been damaged so badly on my right side that when I put a phone on that ear, I cannot hear a thing. The doctors said I probably won't ever get my hearing back.

"All the feeling is gone from the left side of my face. The doctors said they cannot predict if or when the nerve damage there will return to normal.

"That's what 'Brother Mark' did to me," I added.

Sheila's voice was sad as she started to speak. "Maria, I am so sorry. I did not know that Mark was abusive, and I did not know what he had done to you."

Her voice suddenly became loud. "No. Don't go back to him! Not ever! A real brother would not treat a sister that way, and I will tell him that the next time I see him!"

Mark kept on calling me for several months, but he never asked anyone else to call me after that day.

Mark informed me that Leta and Hasana had managed to get out of the yard at his sister's house. They ran away and were never located afterwards. I knew he was sorely disappointed, but my days of feeling sorry for him were over.

Once, he had asked me the name of the hospital my mother was in so that he could send her a card. He lied. He called her at the hospital and spent the whole call asking her to persuade me to come back to him.

I was so upset that the next time he called me, all my disgust for him erupted into several minutes of hollering. Before I hung up, I forbade him to ever call my mother again. I remembered the wife who called him, screaming that he would never see his son. Mark managed to have that effect on the women who had loved him, and he still didn't understand why.

Chapter 37

CONQUERORS

It was now the evening of December 31, 1974. New Year's Eve. Before Dad, Richard, and I left home, we got a call from an aunt with an update on my cousin Kirk in Buffalo. He had gotten involved in the jazz scene in his hometown, and he was living the life of a model citizen. While working on his associate's degree, he had been asked to help teach music classes in one of their community colleges. That report literally had me smiling all during our short trip to church.

We reached our light-colored, stone church just a few minutes before the start of the Watch Meeting service. I didn't give a testimony every year, but this year had been radically different for me. Somebody might have had a rough year like I had. They needed to know that they could make it.

When Watch Meeting started that night, there were about 25 people seated in the sanctuary. Three older deacons stood in front of the pulpit and announced that we would begin our testimony service. One of those deacons began a slow, raspy version of the song, *"I Will Trust In the Lord."* My brother was on the piano. The organist joined the song in the middle of the first verse and picked up the beat, so it morphed into a happy declaration.

A woman stood up at her seat after a couple of verses, waiting for the song to end. This was a sign that she wanted to give her testimony. Nobody would start a new song while another person was standing. I quickly stood up to claim my place as the second testimony.

Some of my thoughts about the past several months came back to me as I stared at the wood-paneled choir stand, waiting my turn. I thought about the previous New Year's Eve and how I had sipped wine with Mark. I was glad I was not doing that this year.

The first woman finished her testimony and sat down.

I started my testimony by saying, "This has been the worst year—really the worst year and a half—ever for me." A few people sitting in front of me turned around to look at me. I heard a baritone, male voice say, "Help her, Lord!"

I am sure the church members have been curious. Some have probably even made up stories to satisfy their curiosity, but I haven't told any of them what transpired with Mark. Can I actually say it now?

I went on. "Both of my grandmothers died...."

I sniffed, thinking about what had happened next.

"....My marriage fell apart...."

More heads turned toward me as my voice weakened. An elderly female voice piped up, "Pray, church!" Another female voice interjected, "Lord, Lord!"

That's all I was going to say about my marriage. The next part hurt just as badly.

"My mother got sick and died."

God, you know I am still torn up about that! Please help me not to cry, not here, not in the middle of my testimony.

I took a deep breath and kept on. "Then two weeks after her funeral, my grandfather suddenly dropped dead from a heart attack." *Gan-Gan, Muz, Mama, Boon-Boon—all dying within months of each other.*

There was total silence in the church. I hesitated again. *There is so much I can't speak of yet. What can I say about 1974 that doesn't leave such a dismal declaration on the year?*

That's when all the good things of the year raced through my mind.

God sending my father to Atlanta on just the right day, so I could escape from Mark.

No cork on my face—ever!

The tiny surgical scar under my eye that nobody seemed to notice.

The feeling on one side of my face that had actually returned after six months.

My recovery from surgery so that I could take over cooking and cleaning just as declining health overtook both my parents.

God honoring my prayer that, if He just had to take Mama, He wouldn't let her die in pain.

Paying my hospital bills because I got another job so that welfare didn't have to pay them.

The nightmares that had finally stopped.

I couldn't tell the people all of that good stuff yet. Still, I had to give a word of encouragement to anybody facing obstacles in the new year.

"This year," I said as I lightly thumped my fist on the back of the wooden pew ahead of me, "This year has been a year of enormous disappointments. And yet, this same year has also been one of enormous blessings! If you're facing troubles, please know that the very God who got me through this kind of year with my sanity still intact will get you through whatever you're facing in 1975!"

I sat down as random voices shouted out or murmured affirmations like "Amen!," "Thank you, Lord," and "He's a good God!" Instead of being buoyed by those encouragements, I felt a sense of sadness.

A woman stood and raised up the song *"Trouble In My Way."* By this time, the drummer had arrived and joined in. The song became a peppy affirmation that Jesus would fix any trouble that comes our way. I sang along while asking myself why my testimony left me feeling disappointed.

It's because I cannot tell about my experience with Mark yet. I am ashamed of it but, even if I weren't, I cannot explain why a woman goes back to an abusive situation. I don't even know how to convince her not to do that…how to save her from finding out that it only gets worse.

Not only that, but I also don't know how to encourage her family to keep praying for her and to work with her if she keeps making that same, dumb move over and over again. How do you help them know when they're doing the best thing, or when they've just become enablers to her repeated bad decisions?

And which woman here is going through an abusive home life and needs to know that somebody understands and cares enough to pray with her? Who doesn't have a family to run to and feels locked into her situation? Who thinks she has no alternative, but to stay with her abuser? Who is dating an abusive man and thinks that he will stop his actions if they get married, or if she forgives him? Which woman will meet a man this coming year and needs to know that he has signs of an abusive personality? I learned those lessons the hard way, and my eyes are clearly open as to what to look out for. However, none of these women will know they have a chance for a better life. . . just because I am too embarrassed to talk about my experience.

Yes, telling the whole ugly story might be the only way to help women avoid the horrors I have faced. I have to find the strength to do that someday.

Just not this day.
Not this year.
But, Lord, someday, I will!

Epilogue

As far as I am concerned, God turned into good what you meant for evil,

- Genesis 50:20a

As awful as my experience was with Mark Towns, if he had not treated me so poorly I would have never returned to Columbus and met Charles D. Scott, III. In 1977, Scott and I married, raised three wonderful children, and had a very interesting life, full of love, laughter, and growth. In 2008, my children and I surrounded Scott's bedside as he left this earthly life for Heaven.

During all those years, I never gave any thought as to what happened to Mark Towns. It was only when I was doing research for this book that I accidentally learned he had died in 2013. My first thoughts? *Lord, why did a person like Mark live longer than a loving and supportive man like Scott?* I got the answer after doing further investigation. That's when I learned that, unlike Scott, Mark Towns died the way he ended up living…all alone, surrounded by no one.

[A] man will always reap just the kind of crop he sows!

- Galatians 6:7b

Startling Statistics about Abuse

(There are many more statistics available. Google "intimate partner violence statistics" for details on these and other statistics.)

1. Every day in the United States, an average of 3 women die from domestic violence.[1]

2. 1 in 4 women will suffer severe abuse at the hands of an intimate partner in her lifetime.[2]

3. 32,000 full-time jobs. That's the equivalent of the 8 million paid work days that women lose every year in the U.S. because of abuse from current or former intimate partners.[3]

---

1   Vagianos, Alanna. "30 Shocking Domestic Violence Statistics That Remind Us It's An Epidemic." *The Huffington Post*, TheHuffingtonPost.com, 23 Oct. 2014, www.huffingtonpost.com/2014/10/23/domestic-violence-statistics_n_5959776.html.

2   *Ibid.*

3   *Ibid.*

4. Domestic violence tends to increase in severity and to occur more often over time.[4]

5. Domestic violence does not depend on the race, culture, socio-economics, or beliefs of the participants.[5]

6. The most dangerous time for the abused party is when she tries to leave the relationship.[6]

---

[4] "Salida, Buena Vista and Poncha Springs Colorado - Domestic Violence Myths." *The Alliance*, alliancechaffee.org/about-domestic-violence/domestic-violence-myths/.

[5] *Ibid.*

[6] "50 Obstacles to Leaving: 1-10." *The National Domestic Violence Hotline*, 10 June 2013, www.thehotline.org/2013/06/10/50-obstacles-to-leaving-1-10/

Discussion Questions

1. Which characters did you like/dislike the most and why?

2. What could Maria have done to keep from being lonely in Atlanta? Did her loneliness impact her willingness to stay in the relationship with Mark?

3. Did Maria's life as a pastor's child have any effect on her behavior as a young adult? If so, how?

4. How did Maria try to get away from Mark after each of the abuse episodes in the book? Why were her efforts ineffective?

5. Maria sought the advice of a minister who said that she and Mark just needed to get married to solve the abuse problem. What do you think would make a person recommend marriage to a woman has been abused by her boyfriend?

6. Why do women return to abusive partners and possible death, disability, or disfigurement? What advice from relatives or friends could persuade them to stay away?

7. Are women adequately prepared to assess the likelihood of physical or mental abuse in a partner?

8. As parents raising young boys, what behaviors might we stress to help prevent them from becoming a person like Mark?

Acknowledgments

First, I'd like to acknowledge God, who wouldn't let me publish anything else until I finally told this whole story. He has someone whom He wants to save from an abusive relationship, and I am honored to be used as His instrument.

Secondly, I would like to thank you for reading this book. If you have questions or comments for me, please email me at maria@mariajscott.com . If you'd like to help get out the word about abuse to more people, please leave a review or rating on this book using the website of whichever vendor you purchased it from. The review does not have to be long; it just needs to be sincere. If you would do it right now, I would be ever so grateful. This action will increase the odds of the right people finding the book and being impacted by it.

Many people graciously gave of their time in order to ensure that this book would be readable and enlightening. I sincerely appreciate it because they never knew what I, as an unpublished author, might be getting them into! One person was Bill Jurist, who read a very early draft and provided helpful corrections and recommendations. He also volunteered to read a later draft with additional comments.

Josephine Scott gave her insights and was the first to suggest having discussion questions at the back of the book.

Saundra Spencer was sent from God to give me a very positive response, right when I was afraid this "book thing" just wasn't going to work out. If there's such a title as "Book Champion," then she held it, graciously offering tremendous support, encouragement, and her unique perspective as a voracious reader. I could always depend on her to quickly help me with any question I was struggling with. Saundra, you'll never know how vital you were in keeping this project going!

D. Simmons-Corbett is a published author who took time to share her experiences, read the book, encourage my efforts, and give me a promotional shout-out at her own book launch party.

Hanifah Kambon, who had relocated to Atlanta from my hometown, read the book and sent me pages of good suggestions. In addition, Hanifah was especially supportive when I mentioned that I wanted some readers who didn't already know me, so there would be no emotional attachment to the story. She found multiple people, and even arranged for a roundtable discussion about the book with her and her friends when she was visiting locally. Hanifah provided the concept and some ideas for chapter titles centered on popular songs. She also brought in her experience as a book club member and teacher to suggest discussion questions. Mary J. Morton, Debra Odum, and Dania Childress were among those folks whom Hanifah solicited as beta readers. Even though they didn't know me, they took time out of their busy lives to provide great insight and suggestions for the book and the discussion questions.

Wilma Shaw, Cuz, I know it was hard because of our relationship, but thank you for reading and commenting, and for the other potential readers you recommended.

Chris Zeidner was another friend who was very supportive,

and who enlisted several readers and passed along their reactions and feedback. My thanks to Myrt Rule and Tim Walker for their encouraging remarks.

Uffa Schley, you know I called you "Eagle Eyes" because you were meticulous in finding errors in the writing. Not only that, but you responded to my other request for assessments. I appreciated your time and thoughts.

My son, Carver Scott, gave me well-thought-out feedback on the early chapters that he read. He has my gratitude because I know he has strong feelings about this part of my life, even though he wasn't around then.

I want to thank Curtis Brooks, who didn't really know me, but was willing to read my story after we got into a discussion about testimonials at church and how newer generations would not know what they were. He brought back a wealth of good ideas and suggestions, which I was quick to include in the book.

Then there were supporters who took an interest in my efforts and recommended additional resources for me. These people include Sandra Denton, Nia Harrington, Shirley Goins, Chuck Scott, and Cathy Levy.

In naming the chapters, I thought I should use song titles from other eras besides the 1960s and 1970s, because I didn't want the young adults to think that abuse only occurred "back in the day." That's when I asked my daughter, Nia Harrington, to find suitable titles that her demographics would recognize. Thankfully, she also weeded out those songs that I liked, but which had underlying messages that she knew I wouldn't appreciate.

There are several folks who didn't read the book, but gave me feedback on an initial look at the proposed covers. I'm not naming all of you, but I do thank you from the bottom of my heart.

Sincerest thanks to Joylynn Ross for her words of wisdom and information while I went through this new journey called "Self-Publishing." It has truly been an eye-opening adventure.

In 2014, Lenora Banks asked me to prepare and deliver a longer speech than the 7- to 9-minute speeches I usually did. This request came when I was ready to start writing this book, and wondering just how you crank out something longer than the short essays I was accustomed to doing. The experience of writing, trashing, and rewriting that speech over and over again taught me that everything doesn't have to be done on the first draft. I would be okay writing and rewriting this book as many times as it took to convey my message and intent clearly.

Finally, I would be remiss if I didn't mention the extra push and support that I got from the Antioch Writers' Workshop after I'd finished my third draft. Even though I didn't feel qualified to call myself a writer then, they recognized the uncertainty that most of the attendees felt and they had a limitless amount of sound advice and encouragement to offer. In spite of my being an introvert, I found it recharging and enlightening to spend a week with others who were in various stages of writing: to read their stories, to make new friends, to engage in workshops, to learn about more resources, and to hear from those who had been successfully published.

If I've missed anybody in my acknowledgments, please forgive me. I rely on lists a lot and, unfortunately, they sometimes don't seem to be around when I need them. I appreciate everything you did. May God bless you for your help and your understanding.

God certainly knows who you need and when you need them. Thank you to each one for being exactly what I needed!

About the Author

Maria Jordan Scott was born on a hospital elevator in Columbus, Ohio. She and her younger brother became PK's (Pastor's Kids) when her father founded a church in her hometown.

After high school graduation, she attended Fisk University in Nashville, Tennessee for three years. Maria earned her Bachelor of Science degree in Computer and Information Science from The Ohio State University.

Maria calls herself a "genealogy nut", and has traveled the U.S. in search of family information. She also enjoys baking anything sweet, making homemade ice cream, and reading. It was Maria's love for the written word and how it often moved her soul that ultimately led her to display her soul in this book.

Maria hopes her inner thoughts and life experiences breathe life into those who, at one time or another, may have felt broken. With her debut release, *Wanna Go. Wanna Stay: My Journey In A Season Of Abuse*, it is Maria's desire that every person who reads her memoir will seek the power of God in her / his life and begin to walk in strength and courage.

Be sure to visit Maria's website at www.mariajscott.com to learn more about her and her books, and to stay updated on future book releases and tour dates. You can also email Maria at maria@mariajscott.com.

www.ingramcontent.com/pod-product-compliance
Lightning Source LLC
Chambersburg PA
CBHW070425010526
44118CB00014B/1910